rhythm planet

The Great World Music Makers

Tom Schnabel

Foreword by Brian Eno

Universe Publishing, New York

First published in the United States of America in 1998
by UNIVERSE PUBLISHING
A Division of Rizzoli International Publications, Inc.
300 Park Avenue South
New York, NY 10010

98 99 00 01 02/ 10 9 8 7 6 5 4 3 2 1

Grateful acknowledgment is made for permission to quote from interviews published in *Stolen Moments: Conversations with Contemporary Musicians*, © Acrobat Books 1988, for the essays on Astor Piazzolla, Ravi Shankar, and Mercedes Sosa.

Design by Ph.D

Produced and edited by Garrett White and Karen Hansgen, Los Angeles, CA

Printed in Singapore

Library of Congress Cataloging-in-Publication Data

Schnabel, Tom.
Rhythm planet: the great world music makers / Tom Schnabel.
    p.   cm.
paperback ISBN 0-7893-0238-1 / hardcover ISBN 0-7893-0239-X
1. Musicians—Biography. 2. World music—History and criticism.
I.   Title.
ML385.S399 1998
780'.92'2—dc21
[B]   98–30441

contents

foreword by Brian Eno

World Music is not a new phenomenon, but a recent name for a process that has a long history. Rock music, for example, is the product of an earlier invasion of World Music that took place over many generations, before recordings existed as vectors. The impact of African music—and in turn Arabic music piped through West Africa—upon European music created what we all now think of as an indigenous Western form: rock and roll. But rock and roll also finds an ancestor in an even earlier world-music revolution. North African Arabic music—the music of the fifth-century Phoenicians and their adventurous traders—was carried all round the coasts of Europe, resulting in the characteristically arabesque style that we now think of as Celtic music. And this in turn translated into the jigs and reels that formed the basis of bluegrass and country and western music.

So the process of absorption and adaptation in music has been going on for a very long time. And of course, when one culture adopts the musical style of another, they also absorb something of the aesthetic and social values of that culture. What, after all, is the point of listening to music? What does the experience do for us? It's such a fundamental question that no one ever thinks to ask it. The first answer, "We listen because we like it," may seem too trivial to pursue, but it leads to another question: "Why do we like it?" It's an important question here because we want to know what happens to people when they experience music that comes from other cultures. My feeling is that this type of experience has the potential for changing our most fundamental values. I don't just mean this in the literal sense—that if you're enjoying an African record you might think better of Africans as a result—but in a deeper sense, too. I think that if you internalize the musical values of a culture, you also internalize some of the broader values which that culture embraces.

Humans negotiate their way through the world on the basis of many different types of information. The most conspicuous type is technical and scientific—the products of rationality. Such forms of knowledge serve us well in clearly defined situations, but many of the most important situations in which we find ourselves are not of that type. Questions of stance arising within these circumstances are not so susceptible to rational solutions because they are not sufficiently well described, or they are new, or they are far too complex. We need to act, but there is no clear basis upon which to make a decision. We are then thrown onto our other human faculties—our abilities to make good guesses, to experiment, to adapt, to imagine.

What rehearses us in these strange talents? How do we get good at the uniquely human process of imagining—that ability to conceptualize how things could otherwise be? I think this is precisely what we are doing with music and other forms of culture. We feel our way towards other understandings of the real world by following our tastes and fascinations within the constructed worlds of music and art. Those 'false' worlds allow us to surrender for a while to different senses of how things might be—and then to see how we feel about it. If you, like me, loved

a music that embraced parts of the body that other music hadn't reached—I'm thinking here of Elvis and his Pelvis—perhaps what you were doing was reimagining YOURSELF as a being for whom the pelvis and the whole sexual being that went with it was given a renewed importance.

Western classical music, on the other hand, is almost uniquely cerebral; there are very few other musics so far removed from any form of physical participation. The idealized "concert-hall" way of listening to classical music—sitting quietly and not moving about—is very local to our time and culture. It suggests to me a very particular picture of what parts of the human organism should be invited into the process of art-engagement . . . and in this case, it certainly doesn't include the pelvis. That's what I mean by a world picture: a picture not only of what's outside, or what could be outside, but also of what's inside, which things about you are the important things, the things to pay attention to.

World Music invites you to enter other places and stay there for a while, and it invites you to pay attention to different parts of yourself. It doesn't necessarily want to tell a complicated story with beginnings and endings. It's more like saying, "Here is an emotional or physical condition you can take part in, the product of another culture's sense of what feels good, what feels right." Listening to such music broadens the number of possible worlds—the number of possible senses of "rightness"—that you can inhabit in your mind. Engaging in any kind of culture is really a way of exercising this basic ability to imagine and participate in other worlds, to enjoy their logic and balance, to see why things are the way they are within them. We don't know of any animals that do this; it's really a human talent, and it's the thing that makes us capable of the big, complicated cooperative projects we are always undertaking. (And also, incidentally, of deceit.)

World Music elements are popping up everywhere as young people look towards music to furnish them with attitudes and "feels" for the world they're growing into—an unfolding world understood by no one, within which they are the pioneers. I think people are extremely aware, especially when they're younger, that you can live in a different reality through a piece of music, and that by surrendering to it you enter into rich new areas of your psyche that you didn't know about before. Isn't this what we call education? I think so, and surely the most important education for anyone at the moment is the development of a sense of poise and empathy in a multicultural, multiethnic, multi-everything world.

introduction

In college I was sometimes teased for being so serious about music, but I didn't care. I was transported by Bartók, Mahler, and John Coltrane; listening to them enabled me to abandon the familiar and predictable. I discovered visionaries like Debussy, Ravel, Ligeti, and Hindemith, and soon I began to explore the music of other cultures—what we now call World Music. I realized early on that there is a spiritual element in great music that we experience on a deeper level than words, so for me the language barrier inherent in World Music has never been a problem. Indeed, in bypassing the language element and the need to follow the meaning of lyrics, we open the doors to surprise and joy. And of course when we read well-translated lyrics, we often discover rich new views of the world. In many cultures, music is much more than entertainment, serving a number of social and religious functions. Here music is an elixir that helps bring healing and spark transcendental experience.

How can we find delight in music from other cultures? What do we have in common with people whose tongues we don't speak? The process starts with the first rhythm we experience, our mother's heartbeat. With rhythm something very elemental is communicated, something beyond the limitations of language. It is the pulse of life. In traditional African music rhythm ruled, and Africa gave rhythm to the world. It was developed into polyrhythms of amazing complexity and dizzying syncopation. With the African diaspora, created by the slave trade, African music—primarily a music of voices and drums—was syncretized into new fusions of Spanish and Portuguese folk songs, Arabic, Jewish, and other music that we hear today.

My first musical revelation came in high school with a modal track by John Coltrane called "India." After listening to it a few times, I found that the music was putting me into a trance state. It was a pivotal experience. I was indeed on a journey, a search for something deeper than what my life as a middle-class adolescent in a Southern California suburb had to offer. I listened to Ravi Shankar, Eric Dolphy, and other artists who seemed to me to be trying to attain a purer form of being through their music.

In the early 1970s, I spent three years in Paris. I first went there to study literature at the Sorbonne, and later returned after finishing my graduate studies in Comparative Literature at UCLA. Due in part to France's colonial legacy, Paris has long been a hub of African as well as Arab musical activity. While there I discovered many artists I'd never heard in America: Franco and TPOK Jazz, Wadi Al Safi, and Umm Kulthum, among many others. I also listened to the radio, especially to long pieces of Arabic music that for me were filled with exoticism and mystery. I returned to Los Angeles in 1976 for what was supposed to be a brief visit. But several things conspired to keep me in L.A. One of those was radio.

In 1979, I became music director of KCRW, a public radio station based in Santa Monica, California, and the host of a daily three-hour show, "Morning Becomes Eclectic." One day a colleague, Roger Steffens, brought in an album by an African group. I was intrigued. It was unlike

the traditional music I'd heard—*Missa Luba*, Babatunde Olatunji's *Drums of Passion*, and other classics that had been released in the U.S. Here was a new style of urban African music. It grew on me. Together Roger and I produced a one-hour weekly insert called "Morning Becomes Makossa," after the title of Manu Dibango's now classic album. We got records however we could, from small distributors, from listeners traveling to Europe, Africa, and elsewhere. Before long, I was able to regularly feature music from West and South Africa, Asia, Brazil, Japan, and the Middle East, among other places. With groundbreaking albums like King Sunny Ade's *Juju Music*—he'd already recorded over 50 albums in Nigeria before his U.S. debut—and with world tours by him, Touré Kunda, Fela Kuti, and others, people experienced firsthand the excitement of this music, and realized that it was accessible, extremely enjoyable, even liberating. A soulful, spiritual bonding was taking place in America, England, France, and other countries. It was our introduction to a music that flourished with vitality, rhythm, and direct communication.

What we know today as World Music is barely twenty years old. Yet even just out of its teens, World Music illustrates the profound changes of the past century. It is as much about evolving technology as about music—a new and potent blend of traditional music and postwar technology, a cross-pollination of musical idioms that has swept the world. The term "World Music" was coined in England in the early 1980s by music marketers trying to categorize new recordings of music from non-Western cultures. "International," "folk," and "ethnic" didn't fit anymore. Records by Congolese rumba bands recorded in Parisian studios didn't belong next to Tino Rossi, Woody Guthrie, or field recordings of Aboriginal music. As a catch-all category, "World Music" didn't make much more sense than these earlier designations, but it served an important purpose: to identify an emerging music most people didn't know much about.

Not all the elements of World Music are new. But when they are combined, an original fusion arises: a synthesis of traditional styles, modern technology, and contemporary music. Elvis Presley, the Beatles, James Brown, Bob Marley, Madonna, Michael Jackson, and countless others have been absorbed and reinterpreted by musicians trained in other traditions. And it's important to realize that in the developing world, Western music, particularly American rock, is identified with First Amendment freedoms and basic human rights, a potent if fuzzy image of the Land of the Free.

What makes World Music so interesting is the degree to which non-Western cultures have been able to assimilate new influences yet retain their musical uniqueness. Malian music played with electric guitars still has a distinctive Malian rhythm and character. World Music artists can celebrate this uniqueness and preserve it, or they can use it as a springboard to a new contemporary style. People like Armenian *duduk* virtuoso Djivan Gasparyan and Malian Wassolou-style singer Oumou Sangare have preserved older musical traditions. Other artists, like Algeria's Khaled and Cameroon's Manu Dibango, have chosen the second way, forging new styles. The greatness of some, like tango master Astor Piazzolla and the great Spanish guitarist Andrés Segovia, lies in having taken regional styles and secured for them international renown. And finally, others like Senegal's Baaba Maal and the late flamenco singer Camarón de la Isla have artfully mixed in new elements while remaining faithful to ancient musical traditions.

Several advances combined to develop traditional music into what we now call World Music. The radio, though invented a century ago, didn't reach most developing nations until after the Second World War. Wherever it appeared, however, radio introduced people to other music, ideas, and cultural attitudes. Much of Africa didn't have radio stations and radio receivers until the 1940s and 1950s. During this time huge transmitters, located at strategic points around the world, began to broadcast programs like "The Voice of America," bringing American culture to new and eager audiences. Later, portable transistor radios made it possible for large numbers of people to listen for the first time. Even today, there's a thriving business in hand-cranked radios and cassette players in Africa, where batteries are still scarce and expensive.

The next key development in the global dissemination of music was the invention and proliferation of the audio cassette in the early 1970s. The availability of affordable and reproducible cassettes—and the boomboxes to play them—meant that for the first time people everywhere could afford to buy music. For ambitious young musicians in developing countries coming of age during the heyday of the Beatles, there were now accessible ways of hearing new sounds; soon they were combining them with their own. Radios, boomboxes, and cassettes served as technological bridges that connected previously isolated peoples, enabling musics of different cultures to combine and recombine. Africans were inspired and influenced by musical travelers as unlikely as Dolly Parton, Sly Stone, and Jim Reeves. Manu Dibango heard Louis Armstrong and Miles Davis on the radio. Khaled heard the music of Johnny Halliday—France's answer to Elvis—and decided to become a musician. In Mali, Salif Keita was influenced by Latin bands like Cuba's Orquesta Aragón, and Ali Farka Toure by bluesmaster John Lee Hooker. Rubén Blades was inspired by the '50s doo-wop of Frankie Lymon, Milton Nascimento heard and loved Ray Charles, Antonio Carlos Jobim heard Miles Davis's cool jazz and forged the bossa nova style. Every instance bears witness to a voyage of discovery into tantalizing new worlds of sound.

World Music is a citified music and a largely urban phenomenon, witness to a steady migration of musicians and other people from village to metropolis. Entrepreneurs saw new markets emerge during the late 1940s and early 1950s, and built recording studios in Lagos, Accra, Leopoldville (later Kinshasa), Johannesburg, Jakarta, Salvador, and other cities to capture and profit from local talent. Soon there was an explosion of new sounds, as studios, clubs, and movie theaters sprang up in developing urban centers. Paris, London, and Brussels also became major hubs of music production and many African bands migrated there.

By the early 1960s, this musical revolution had completed several cycles. Without question, the various synergistic musical styles created by the African diaspora have been the most influential in our century. African music had first been transmitted to Cuba and the New World by slaves. Now it returned to Africa in myriad new styles. The Congolese rumba of Joseph Kabasele and Franco, which took West Africa by storm, came from the West Africans' love of Cuban bands like Orquesta Aragón and Orquesta Broadway. Musicians like Youssou N'Dour, Manu Dibango, and

Salif Keita have also acknowledged a tremendous debt to Cuban music. Few Cuban bands actually toured in Africa; rather, their music was transmitted via recordings. In the 1950s, some two hundred Cuban 78-rpm recordings on the GV label found their way into various West African countries, and African musicians fell in love with Cuban *son* and *charanga*.

World Music arrived at a propitious time; at the start of the 1980s, many young people were looking for new and interesting sounds. The punk era was winding down, the big rock productions of Yes, Journey, and other bands had become ponderous and predictable. Disco had likewise faded. Jamaican music, from rock steady to ska and reggae, had been popular first in England and then in America during the 1970s, and there was still great interest in reggae music. But two of its giants died prematurely—Bob Marley of cancer in 1980, Peter Tosh murdered just a few years later—and there were no heirs apparent.

Several things happened to crystallize the recognition of World Music. In the early 1980s, in the wake of the record industry recession that began in 1979, many major labels dropped smaller acts, and innovative, independent companies formed to take up the slack. Two landmark albums appeared during this time. In 1981, David Byrne and Brian Eno produced a bestselling album, *My Life in the Bush of Ghosts*, which mixed Lebanese, Egyptian, and other music to create a unique, multilayered sound. In the following year, Island Records' Chris Blackwell, who had introduced reggae to larger audiences with the first crossover records by Marley, produced the domestic release of King Sunny Ade's infectious *Juju Music*. This was a new sound, a blend of traditional Yoruba talking drum rhythms spiced with electric and country and western slide guitars.

In 1982, Peter Gabriel, a charismatic British rock star with a broad range of musical interests, launched WOMAD (World of Music and Dance) in England to present festivals featuring World Music artists alongside established pop acts. He later subsidized the Real World label with profits from his successful solo album, *So* (1986), and has been influential as a World Music producer. Also in 1986, the familiar voice of Paul Simon, singing alongside the South African voices and players on the Grammy-winning *Graceland*, introduced countless new fans to African music. Grateful Dead drummer Mickey Hart brought Deadheads to his Planet Drum concerts, books, and albums. David Byrne, who had incorporated African and other World Music styles into his work with the Talking Heads, founded the Luaka Bop label. Even the Rolling Stones have had a role, with their long-time fascination with reggae and North African music. Currently, they've helped to popularize France's multicultural big band, l'Orchestre National de Barbès, which plays a blend of *rai*, reggae, *Jajouka*, a bit of Hendrix-style guitar, and much else.

World Music has grown consistently and steadily. It was not the "next big thing" that critics and enthusiasts had predicted, nor has World Music yet delivered a megastar on the scale of Madonna or Michael Jackson. Nevertheless, today there are shows every week in major cities in the U.S., Canada, and Europe, featuring artists from every corner of the earth. World Music also has a great ally in film soundtracks. *The Last Temptation of Christ*, *Dead Man Walking*, *Powaqqatsi*, and *Equinox* have introduced such musicians as Nusrat Fateh Ali Khan, Djivan Gasparyan, and Salif Keita to mainstream audiences. Filmgoers who might otherwise never wander into a record store's World Music section can easily buy a soundtrack, which plants a seed for more discoveries. Regrettably, none of the global music television networks have played a role in introducing listeners in the West to the genre.

I have been fortunate to encounter some of World Music's greatest stars, people whose artistry and wisdom deserve more recognition than I could ever give in an ephemeral radio interview. Over the years, their music has broadened my horizons and has been a source of consistent emotional delight and intellectual stimulation. My esteem for them should be obvious in the personal selections that follow. This book allows me to pay tribute to many of the musicians I've been lucky enough to interview, as well as honor some I couldn't.

There are many artists—not necessarily World Music artists—who have moved me deeply. John Coltrane, Miles Davis; the magnificent Lebanese diva Fairuz, innovators like Paco de Lucia and Eddie Palmieri. There are African artists like Franco and Joseph Kabasele, whose music left a giant imprint all over Africa. Some, like King Sunny Ade and the South African diva Miriam Makeba, appeared in my first book, *Stolen Moments*; I've chosen not to include them here, to make room for others.

Almost twenty years after I first became involved in promoting World Music, I know it's here to stay. Over the past decade, World Music has revitalized pop and helped usher in new styles, like ambient, dub, trip hop, and trance, led by England's Loop Guru, William Orbit, Transglobal Underground, Talvin Singh, Jah Wobble, and others. World Music now has its own section in record stores; there are numerous specialized labels, a Billboard chart, and a Grammy category.

In many ways, World Music is the music that best reflects the world as it exists today, perched on the edge of the next millennium. A new multicultural sensibility has emerged in many places—in Los Angeles alone over 80 languages are spoken, reflecting changes taking place in urban centers around the world. People are increasingly interested in the wisdom of other cultures, from the Eastern philosophy of Deepak Chopra to the practice of Chinese medicine and alternative healing. People are turning to World Music for stimulation, knowledge, and even comfort. Interest in sacred music from other cultures has increased, too, and festivals like the World Sacred Music Festival in Fez, Morocco, have bigger audiences each year. Everywhere people seek fresh perspectives from traditions outside of their own, underscoring a shared humanity.

It's been said many times that music is the universal language, the most sublime emanation of the human spirit. I am still awed by its magestic beauty. And I am fortunate to have served the muse and to have shared my passion for music with many people. I hope this book will open your ears—and hearts—to new kinds of musical expression, and help you enjoy them as much as I have.

Tom Schnabel Venice, California July 1998

There are many people who helped to make this book possible. I would first like to thank Tony Cohan of Acrobat Books for his encouragement when the present volume was just an idea. Many thanks go as well to my translators and transcribers: Andrea Ferraz, Catherine Generous, Susan di Giulio, Frédérique Joly, Nan Sheri Lieberman, and Nora Saidi; to the KCRW staff, including Margaret Mendenhall, Sarah Spitz, and Bob Werne; and to KCRW General Manager, Ruth Seymour, for providing me with a radio home from which to share the music of the artists in these pages. I am also grateful to Abel Barboza, Umberto Capiro, Eduardo Citrinblum, Don Cohen, Howard Dratch, Redha Hazourli, Lucina Hubbard, Roberto Lestinge, Paule Micalef, Nnamdi Moweta, Jesús Naranjo, Bob Ramirez, Jasmin Saidi, and Maria Wilson. Thanks to Roger Steffens, who prodded me to feature African music on the radio before others had even dreamed of it. Much love and appreciation to Cherie Chen for her good ideas, editing assistance, and constant encouragement. A special thanks goes to my "Café L.A." producer, Laura Connelly-Schneider, who tracked down many of the photos in this book. I would also like to thank the staff at Universe Publishing, especially Charles Miers, Bonnie Eldon, Sarah Scheffel, and David Brown for all of their hard work and patience. Finally, I owe a great debt to the Ph.D staff and designer Michael Hodgson, whose knowledge and love of World Music brought special insight to the project and to his superb design; to Karen Hansgen and Wendy Sand for their editorial assistance; and to my persevering editor, Garrett White, without whom this book would not have been possible.

Albita

For two long days in spring 1993, in the Mexican town of Juárez across the border from El Paso, Texas, Havana-born singer Albita Rodríguez sat in a Chinese restaurant pondering her future. Should she return to Cuba, or defect to the United States? She made a fateful decision. She and her band walked over the bridge into El Paso, then telephoned Miami. An El Paso radio station raised the money to send them east, and within a year the singer had been taken under the wing of producer Emilio Estefan, husband of Gloria Estefan. Celebrity-studded crowds flocked to see her at Centro Vasco, a popular Cuban-owned restaurant and club in Miami's Little Havana. By 1997, she was at the White House, draped in black velvet, serenading Bill and Hillary Rodham Clinton.

Known professionally by her first name only, Albita loves the old *guajiras* and *sons*, the Cuban folk music she grew up with. When she talks, she seems quintessentially Cuban, yet she challenges the role of female singers in the macho world of Latin music. She has often adopted an androgynous look, her hair cut short and sometimes dyed platinum; she favors Versace and Armani threads. She has appeared in *Newsweek*

It never occurred to me that I'd have to enter a country illegally. It makes you feel like a delinquent when you're not. It's an experience you never forget. The one thing that helps you to live with it is to know that others have suffered through much worse. The respect you feel for their lives makes you feel better about your own.

and the *New York Times*, and modeled for French *Vogue*. Albita's come a long way from that apprehensive 30-year-old singer sitting in a Chinese restaurant in Juárez.

When I interviewed her in summer 1996, Albita was in Los Angeles to perform a spectacular show with Celia Cruz, Tito Puente, El Gran Combo de Puerto Rico, El General, and Eddie Palmieri—the biggest Latin show of the year. I asked her if the thought of performing before a crowd of some 15,000 made her nervous. "Always," she answered. "I get nervous before every show, no matter what it is. But with this type of show, with so many well-known singers of that caliber, I'm even more nervous."

In the 1970s, Albita performed in bands that specialized in guajira-style country music, but she was also playing the rock music her peers were listening to—bands such as Led Zeppelin, Chicago, and Blood, Sweat, and Tears. Her original compositions combine Cuban classics and traditional rhythms arranged with the contemporary flavor of rock and jazz. I asked her about her musical idols. "There are many," she says. "Ramón Velóz, Trio Matamoros, Los Van Van, Irakere, and all the music that was part of the Cuban *nueva canción* movement—all of that movement, not just Silvio Rodríguez, but also Miriam Ramos, Noël Nicola, Sintesis, lots of people. I'm really blessed. I say

'blessed' because I think it's a blessing to be able to listen to a lot of music. I listen to anything I can get my hands on. I don't limit myself to any particular genre or style or form. Quite the contrary. My parents [well-known *punto guajiro*—acoustic country— singers] were my first great influence. Like everyone, I like the Beatles, and also all the Cuban music that was being produced at that time. Guajira is just a small part of Cuban country music. Guajira is the style of how a composer living in the city sees the country. I played all types of country music, especially in the early years."

Soon, however, she found herself caught in the middle. Younger musicians thought that her musical style was too old, and older musicians considered her too avant-garde. I asked Albita why she left Cuba. "Like so many other Cubans," she says, "I was looking for my own space, reaching out for my freedom, the feeling that I was my own person and, above all, the ability to make decisions about my personal and professional life. Even more important was the fact that I didn't want to be part of the game there."

She describes her experience of crossing the border as "horrible." "I never imagined that I would have to do that," she says. "It never occurred to me that I'd have to enter a country illegally. It makes you feel like a delinquent when you're not. It's an experience that

you never forget. The one thing that helps you to live with it is to know that others have suffered through much worse. The respect you feel for their lives makes you feel better about your own."

Albita eventually brought her parents to Miami. They miss everything about Cuba, as does Albita. "That's where my whole life was," she says, "where I spent my childhood, my youth, where my friends are, my neighborhood, where I had my first guitar. It was my whole life for thirty years. It's as though someone has torn off a piece of my body."

Her androgynous image—which includes, at times, men's clothes, suspenders, pomaded short hair—has attracted a great deal of attention here in both the straight and the gay press, as well as in fashion magazines. Occasionally it seems as if more attention is paid to her clothes and hairstyle than to her music. "I don't mind," she says. "Of course I'd prefer that people pay attention to my music. When I'm on stage, I'm not even trying to send a particular message. I'm just trying to entertain the people who have come to see me. I've been like this since I was born—

short, skinny, ugly, with no butt, no hips, and small breasts. I'm not your typical Latin woman. I'm very different." She laughed when I told her that she was much more attractive in person than she already is in her photographs. "Thank you," she said. "I hope I'm more attractive in person, since photographs can't speak. God didn't give me much physically, but at least he gave me the ability to express myself well."

The press has often compared Albita to artists who have nothing to do with Latin music: k.d. lang, Lotte Lenya, Edith Piaf. She is flattered, of course, at being compared to some of the best voices in the world. "One day," she says, "I hope to claim at least a small amount of their notoriety and their talent." Madonna has said that Albita is the best thing to come out of Cuba since flan. "If Madonna ever decides to charge me for the publicity that she's given me," Albita says, "I'll never be able to pay. For the short time that I've known her, she's been wonderful. She's marvelous. She's paid a lot of attention to me, and I'll always be thankful to her."

Rubén Blades

Rubén Blades is among the most versatile and universally respected of Latin stars. A *salsero* poet writing songs about common people and their plight, he is also an actor in films and on Broadway, a Harvard Law School graduate, and a politician who founded his own party and made an impressive run for the presidency of his native Panama in 1994. Through it all, he has remained one of the most successful Latin musicians on the scene.

Blades makes salsa with a thinker's edge. His fans see him as a leader of the *nueva canción* (new song) movement, a powerful mix of poetry, rhythm, and socially conscious themes. His lyrics are unlike most of what you'll find in salsa music. I had long wanted to interview him, but hadn't been able to connect with his busy schedule. I finally did meet him, but not in the way I imagined. In 1995, he moved into an L.A. neighborhood not far from mine, and I invited him to dinner. The first of several conversations began there, and I later invited him into the station for a live interview.

Blades was born in Panama City on July 16, 1948, the son of a Cuban mother and a Colombian-born Panamanian father, also named Rubén Blades. His paternal grandfather

> I understand why a lot of people hesitate before becoming involved in politics, because it's one of the dirtiest scenarios you can find in terms of highlighting the worst in human nature. It's unbelievable what they'll do! [My opponents] invented the craziest things.

was English, hence the surname Blades, which can be pronounced "Blades" (as in razor blades) or "Blah-dess." He was raised in a working-class neighborhood of Panama City called Caraquilla, and he looks back on his childhood there with respect and gratitude. "Some areas were poorer than others," he recalls, "but in general everyone had the work ethic—you know, everyone went to school, everyone wanted to make their families proud. We were poor, but we were not abandoned, we were not dirty, and we were not hoodlums. I'm very happy that I got to grow up in such an environment."

Blades points to his family as the source of his iconoclasm, as well as his daring to be good at many things. His mother was an actress and an accomplished pianist and singer, and his father was a bongo player who became a detective. His paternal grandmother seems to have been a particularly great inspiration. She was a vegetarian and a devotee of yoga, practices not exactly common for Panamanians of her generation. She crusaded for women's rights and, with limited funds for her children's education, decided that it would be best to send the girls to university before the men. She was way ahead of her time, and Blades credits her with having given him the confidence to back up his convictions at an early age.

"I grew up in a household with very strong women," Blades says. "My mother was a singer and an excellent piano player, as well

as a radio and soap opera actress. So I probably get my desire for acting through her. Emma Bosquez, my father's mother, was an extraordinary woman. She married twice and divorced twice. She was born in 1895, and in the 1920s, to be divorced was looked upon with derision, especially in a society controlled by men like Panama. She would not take any money from her husbands, and she didn't have enough to send all four kids to school, so she sent the women first and taught the men at home. She fought for the vote for women and was arrested. She painted, she was a poet, and she was one of the first women in Panama to graduate from high school—at a time when there were no universities. She taught me how to read when I was about four, and talked to me about Cubism. She was a very interesting woman, and it was she, I think, who created in me the desire to become a lawyer. Her search for justice inspired me."

Though Blades studied law and passed the bar exam in Panama, music was always his muse. American and British rock and roll of the '50s and '60s triggered his decision to become a musician, especially the great '50s doo-wop music of Frankie Lymon ("Why do Fools Fall in Love") and, later, the Beatles. He saw Frankie Lymon & the Teenagers in a '50s movie called *Rock, Rock, Rock* and said to himself, "If he can do that, I can do that." Seeing the group play a hugely successful concert in Panama sealed his determination. He was still in high school when he began to sing with a local group called The Saints, covering Beatles staples such as "And I Love Her" and other pop fare like "Strangers in the Night" and "Last Train to Clarksville."

Later, Blades used many of these elements to alter the basic sound of salsa by introducing synthesizers, doo-wop, and other non-standard ingredients. He also departed from standard lyrics about unrequited love to write songs about gangsters, Oliver North, and injustice in Latin America, often using language that borrowed elements from the fiction of Jorge Luis Borges, Gabriel García Márquez, and other modern Latin American writers.

Blades never practiced law in his native country. Instead, he moved to New York in 1974 and found a job—in the mailroom and sweeping the floors—at Fania Records, the great Latin music label founded by the late Gerry Masucci. His career began two years later with trombonist Willie Colón's band, with whom he transformed salsa by writing and singing songs with difficult arrangements and keen social commentary. In 1978, he recorded *Siembra* with Colón, which became his first big hit and one of the most popular salsa albums of the decade. In 1982, after three memorable albums with Colón, Blades went on to form his own band, Seis del Solar, with whom he won two Grammys.

In 1983, he was invited to speak to the Inter-American Association at Harvard about music and its impact on society and on Latin America. "Some students came forward after the talk," he recalls, "and said, 'What about coming here to study?' I said, 'Sure, send me the application and I'll consider it.' And they did. I sent it back, and I was accepted." At the pinnacle of his success, Blades abruptly put his career on hold to attend Harvard Law

School, pursuing a degree in International Law. "At the time I was becoming, I think, too complacent, too comfortable," he continues. "I was doing very well in my music. All of a sudden, everybody wanted to interview me. And I said, 'You know, this is the perfect time to take a break and go into something really difficult, where I have absolutely no control.' But boy was it hard. About six weeks into it, I said, 'Why did I do this?!' But I'm very, very happy that I went through it."

Blades's stubborn individualism and his music's social statements didn't make him popular with everyone. One of his most remarkable songs is about the death of Father Romero, slain by a right-wing assassin's bullet in El Salvador ("Father Antonio and Andrés the Altar Boy," on *Buscando America*). It embodies some of the most trenchant social commentary ever written by a salsero. "I was in New York at the time," Blades says, recalling the genesis of the song, "and I was very angry about what was going on in Central America, the loss of life, the lies that were being told about the situation there. In those days, my anger just took me to writing songs. When Romero, the archbishop, was killed, I was so incensed that I felt I should write a song and include it on *Buscando America*, which was an effort to make everyone aware of what was going on, and to try to voice a position for those who could not speak. It's one of the songs that I really have a special affection for."

Blades is a Renaissance man, with Old World manners and a romantic temperament, yet he has proven capable of addressing, both as a musician and as a politician, the concerns of ordinary people. He started his own political party, Papa Egoro (a Panamanian Indian term meaning Mother Earth), and made an unsuccessful bid for the presidency of Panama in 1994. With 18 percent of the popular vote, Blades narrowly missed coming in second, fighting slur campaigns accusing him of being a CIA operative, a communist, an embezzler, and so on.

I asked Blades if his success as a musician and an actor was a liability or an asset when it came to running for president. "In a sense it helped," he said. "I had name recognition. We didn't have money, but people knew who I was. On the other hand, I had been known primarily as a musician, and later on as an actor, and people said, 'Well, this guy's crazy. He wants to come in here now and become president because he sings, and he's been away for twenty years.' I participated in five televised debates with the other candidates. And after ten, fifteen, twenty public opportunities to present the proposals of the movement, the direction I thought Panama should take, people started saying, 'Okay, this guy is, in fact, a politician. He can lead, politically.' But they didn't say that until after the debates. So it helped me in one way, and it was a bit of a hindrance in another."

When the Northridge earthquake hit Los Angeles in January 1994, Blades took the first flight home to be with his wife, Lisa. Though their home was in Santa Monica, one of the areas hardest hit by the quake, it escaped major damage. He returned to Panama soon after, again encountering an opposition that tried to paint him as a salsa singer interested in Hollywood rather than a political reformer bent on returning Panama to a legitimate and honest democracy. "At one point during the election, it came out in the headlines in Panama that I was a U.S. citizen, and another time that my Harvard diploma was phony. I understand why a lot of people hesitate before becoming involved in politics, because it's one of the dirtiest scenarios you can find in terms of highlighting the worst in human nature. It's unbelievable what they'll do! [My opponents] invented the craziest things. Still, we did well, and I'm glad I set out to do what I said I would do."

After losing the election, Blades didn't go into mourning. He immediately resumed a hectic pace in both music and acting. His first major film role had come in 1985 with *Crossover Dreams*, in which he played a Latino boxer trying to succeed in America. That first role was followed by parts in, among others, *The Milagro Beanfield War*, *Mo' Better Blues*, *The Two Jakes*, *The Color of Night*, and *City of Angels*.

Over the years, he has developed a reputation as a versatile actor. He was never formally trained, having come to acting through his music. He considers himself lucky, especially given the general shortage of good roles for Latinos. "I've worked with a lot of good people," he says. "Of all the films I have worked on, *Dead Man Out*, with Danny Glover, stands out. That was the first time I really had to reach as an actor. I played a death-row inmate, and Danny Glover played a psychiatrist. It was about the morality of the death penalty. I'm very proud of that role."

I asked Blades if he could define the key to his success in so many different fields. "Perhaps the most defining aspect of my character," he says, "came from my family's desire to pursue different careers and different goals. No one ever told me that I couldn't do something myself. I was always encouraged to try— I grew up thinking that the definition of failure is not to try."

Umm Kulthum

Nicknamed "The Great Pyramid of Arabic Music," Umm Kulthum is considered by many to have been the greatest singer of the Arab world. From the 1940s to the 1960s, her voice wafted out of Cairo cafés, homes, and offices during weekly noon radio concerts. The entire city slowed so that people could hear the broadcasts with a minimum of interruption. Gamal Abdel Nasser used Kulthum's nationalist songs to keep the public behind his Pan Arabist campaigns, and President Anwar Sadat once gave a national address on the same day as her radio concert and wound up without an audience (a mistake he was never to repeat). A legend in her own lifetime, Kulthum is held in the highest esteem by Egyptians from all walks of life, from Nobel laureate Naguib Mahfouz to teenagers on the streets of Cairo.

Umm Kulthum was born in 1904 into a peasant family in a poor section of the northeast Nile delta. She was given her first voice lessons by her father, an Islamic cantor who sang Koranic verses in her village. As a young girl, she had to dress as a boy to escape notice by the religious authorities when she recited verses from the Koran in cafés. Kulthum learned to sing them with great skill and fluency, eventually becoming a perfectionist in both diction and enunciation, qualities important in Arab singing. She was later renowned for her love songs, which sometimes lasted for more than an hour. Listeners were driven into a frenzy. She was once asked to repeat a particularly beautiful line fifty-two times, which she did, all the while embellishing and ornamenting the phrase, drawing the audience into rhapsodic paroxysms of joy.

In addition to her marvelous phrasing and vocal ornamentation, Kulthum possessed a powerful voice, reported to have once shattered drinking glasses. She injected all of her songs with *shaggan*, or emotional yearning, another important element in Arabic song. After her death in February 1975, more than three million people joined her funeral cortège through the streets of Cairo. Even now, on the first Thursday of every month, Egyptian radio stations rebroadcast her famous radio concerts.

ARAB FILM DISTRIBUTION PRESENTS

She had the musicality
of Ella Fitzgerald,
the public presence of
Eleanor Roosevelt,
and the audience of
Elvis Presley.

Umm Kulthum,
A VOICE LIKE EGYPT

A film narrated by Omar Sharif

directed by Michal Goldman, produced by Michal Goldman and Barbara Holecek, cinematography by Kamal Abd al-Aziz
Based on the book "The Voice of Egypt": Umm Kulthum, Arabic Song, and Egyptian Society in the 20th Century, by Virginia Danielson
A production of the Filmmakers Collaborative funded in part by the National Endowment for the Humanities and The Ford Foundation

ARAB FILM
DISTRIBUTION

Manu Dibango

African superstar Emmanuel "Manu" Dibango, saxophonist, pianist, singer, composer, and arranger, was born in 1933 in Douala, Cameroon, the son of a high-ranking civil servant and a dressmaker. Dibango has always been a modernist with a big vision, and he has scored many firsts. On his breakthrough album *Soul Makossa* (1973), he became the first musician to combine elements of American soul and funk with traditional African music, creating a sound that was both thoroughly African and contemporary. "Soul Makossa" was the first African single to hit the U.S. top 40, earning a gold record and a Grammy nomination, and establishing Dibango's reputation almost overnight. His early hits helped to internationalize African music, and they have influenced all of it in their wake, including the music of Zap Mama, Angelique Kidjo, and Les Têtes Brulées, to name just a few. During the 1980s, Dibango recorded cutting-edge albums with producer Bill Laswell, and he has worked with artists like Herbie Hancock, the Fania All-Stars, Fela Kuti, Don Cherry, and Nicky Skopelitis. With the release of *Polysonik* in

We listened to jazz in
St.-Germain-des-Prés.
I fell in love with
Armstrong, Ellington,
Sidney Bechet, Count
Basie. That was the first
time we Africans saw
blacks with a positive
image as artists.

1991, Dibango became the first African musician to record a hip-hop album.

Dibango has always been a forward-looking musician able to successfully incorporate international trends while maintaining a creative base faithful to West African pop. As a young Cameroonian musician in the 1940s, however, Dibango didn't have access to much music. "There was no radio at that time," he recalls. "But we used to listen to music on record players, and also to church music. My mother conducted the choir in church, so I started to sing by age five. I had one uncle who played traditional guitar. So somewhere between the church, the village, and the city, you find Manu Dibango."

On the side, Dibango also listened to French pop music and other sounds forbidden in his strict household. As a teenager in the 1940s, he attended performances in the port city of Douala by African musicians playing in traditional as well as contemporary styles. Listening to these bands, he was exposed to the roots of the music that would become the Cameroonian *makossa* style, a variant of Congolese, Central African, and West African Highlife music. Highlife music originated in the colonial Africa of the 1920s, and fused European instruments and musical styles with African elements. The name Highlife came from the adoption, especially by the urban African elite, of the practice of dressing up for a night on the town—"stylin'"—in emulation of the European upper-class lifestyle. Highlife music played an important role in the development of urban African musical styles, and its influence was felt from the ballroom dance bands preferred by the coastal elite to rural guitar bands.

In 1949, at age 15, Dibango was sent to school in Paris, where his musical awakening really began. "I was lucky," he says, recalling his childhood. "My parents loved me very much. They gave me the maximum they could give me. They sent me to Paris to learn. At that time, we were still colonized, and it was not like emigrating, but more like going to the capital. When I came to France, I was no stranger. I was a Frenchman—an African Frenchman. My parents wanted me to be a philosophy professor, so I studied that of course. But I knew that I was a musician, and I was also taking piano lessons."

In Paris, he was exposed to many kinds of music, but especially to American jazz, which was then all the rage. "How happy I was to hear Louis Armstrong humming on Parisian radio," he recalls. "Here was a black voice singing tunes that reminded me of those I had learned in church. There was a Latin scene at that time, but there was not yet any talk of African music. All of the Africans in Paris were students. We listened to jazz in St.-Germain-des-Prés. That is how I fell in love with Armstrong, Ellington, Sidney Bechet, Count Basie—all the fantastic people coming there. And I was more and more involved in this instead of philosophy. That was the first time we Africans saw blacks with a positive image as artists."

In the 1950s, Dibango played in jazz clubs and cabarets in Paris and Brussels. It was in Brussels that he met the father of Congolese music, Joseph Kabasele, "Le Grand Kalle," who was there with a political delegation negotiating the Belgian Congo's transition to self-rule as Zaire. Dibango joined Kalle's band, African Jazz, and left Brussels for Kinshasa for a two-month stay that would last two years. Congo won its independence from Belgium, and Kabasele recorded "Independence Cha Cha" and "Africa Mokili Mobimba," which became not only major African hits but also anthems celebrated by all newly independent African nations, as well as those trying to achieve independence. Dibango recorded more than one hundred songs with the group.

"Listen to 'Indépendence Cha Cha,'" Dibango says, "then you can have the flavor of what was going on. They were dealing with the Cuban-African rumba and traditional Congolese music. At that time, Kinshasa had the most powerful radio station in French-speaking Africa. It was very funny, because in [Cameroon], the radio stopped at ten o'clock at night. But Radio Kinshasa played until four o'clock in the morning. So everybody was listening to Congolese music. It was very popular all over Africa."

Dibango's first straight makossa recording was *Nasengina*, released in 1964. Around this time, he also took a greater interest in American soul, and he began to gain renown as a saxophonist rather than as a pianist. In 1968, he recorded the eponymous *Manu Dibango*, which contained the seeds of his mature philosophy of African music, illustrating and resolving old quarrels between traditional and modern styles. Dibango mixes both in his music, and he has never seen any conflict between them. "You have two-way traffic between town and village, village and town," he writes in his preface to Graeme Ewens's *Africa O-ye!* "You have a sound that arrives in the town and returns to the village, changed. The echo which comes back is not the same as the original. When a note arrives in town from the village, the town returns it with electronic delay, with reverb, limiter, and all that studio technology, but it is the same note that came from the village. . . . Now everyone knows the modern music. And even the folklore music is moving. Traditional musicians are human, they live in the modern world, and their music is not fixed, it changes. Traditional music has definitely been affected by modern music, because the same people listen to both. The tradition will always be there, of course, but like a person, it evolves, develops. Just as fishermen still use canoes, they now have canoes fitted with outboard motors."

Dibango has been a powerful force in the modernization of African music. His international hit, "Soul Makossa," was the first to fuse American soul music with African sounds. The song had an unlikely beginning. "My musical story is linked to soccer," he says. "There was a big African Cup in Cameroon in 1972, and [I was] asked to write music [for it]—a march. I wrote 'Makossa,' for the B-side. Then we lost the cup, and no one wanted to listen anymore, no A-side, no B-side. At the end of '72, some talent scouts came from America. They were black Americans. They wanted to sell African music in America. They came to France, and there was 'Soul Makossa.' They went back to America, and this song became what everybody knows now."

Soul Makossa sold more than a million copies. "Makossa was not a traditional dance," Dibango explains. "It's a city music, an urban music, mostly in Cameroon. Cameroon is between West Africa and Central Africa. We can say that we are close to Nigeria in one part and we are close to Congo in the other part, which gives us at least two possibilities, musically speaking. There was this Afrobeat and Juju music coming from Nigeria on one side, and on the other side, what we call Rumba-Congolese. If you add the Cameroonian personality to these two musics, you have makossa. There is happiness, love, everything in the music. And if there is a message, it is a message that comes from the feet to the head. First you must dance."

Dibango scored another first with the release of his 1991 recording *Polysonik*, this time mixing hip hop with African music. His 1994 *Wakafrica*, brilliantly produced by George Acogny, features guest performers including Salif Keita, Peter Gabriel, Youssou N'Dour, Sinead O'Connor, and Ladysmith Black Mambazo. Dibango's ability to draw such impressive and diverse talent is testimony to his high standing among other artists, and his proven ability to stay on the cutting edge of African music.

I asked him what he thinks about when he imagines African music. "Well, we usually say African musics," he says, "because Africa is a continent. From Senegal to Cape Town, I'm

telling you, there is a nice trip. Each country has its own flavor. Each country has its own way to play this six-eight we have in common, and the pentatonic scale we share throughout Africa. And the voice—there are lots of colors, from Youssou N'Dour to Papa Wemba going on to Angola with [Kuenda] Bonga. This is a fantastic trip. "

After such a rich and varied career, I was curious to know who his biggest inspirations have been. "That's a very difficult question," he says. "I began by listening to church music. So, I'll start with that. After that, Duke Ellington is one of my favorites, and then we go to Tchaikovsky and then back to African music. I cannot name just one or two. If you like music, you must like all music. You cannot say you like this instead of that. So, once in a while I like Duke, once in a while I like Miriam Makeba, once in a while I like John Coltrane, once in a while James Brown, once in a while Youssou N'Dour. When you listen to music, if it inspires you, that's good music for you."

Manu Dibango   31

Djavan

Known for a voice of aching tenderness and fragility, Djavan is part of the so-called MPB (*música popular brasileira*) generation that came of age in the late 1960s. His songs have been covered by Gal Costa, Caetano Veloso, Nana Caymmi, and other top Brazilian artists. But unlike Veloso, who wrote surrealist lyrics, or Gilberto Gil, who wrote more overtly political songs, Djavan focuses on love songs, written and sung with honesty and humility. With simple language and a voice of tremendous subtlety, he communicates something of the joy and pain of love.

Djavan (pronounced Dee-jah-van) was born Djavan Caetano Viana in 1949 in Maceió, a town in Brazil's northeastern state of Alagoas. "It's a very poor state," he says. "At the same time, like other northeastern states—Bahia, Pernambuco, Ceará—Alagoas has a really rich folklore tradition, with a powerful African influence. It was there that I grew up musically, hearing folk music and listening to my mother sing. My mother loved to sing; she had an African way of singing."

Djavan's father died when he was only five years old. With little information about his ancestry, he drew inspiration from his mother. "I don't know exactly what her connection was to the history of the slaves," he says. "What I do know is that she had a real African spirit. She sang all day long and danced. There were three of us, and she made up lullabies to put each of us to sleep. She was very creative, my mother. She was a beautiful negress, very inspired and beguiling."

By 1973, Djavan was covering Beatles songs in Maceió with his band, LSD. "I was also composing," he recalls, "but in Maceió they didn't accept my music. They thought my stuff was strange." That same year, he set out for the first time on the two-and-a-half-day bus ride to Rio. He arrived with nothing but hope, a guitar, and the clothes on his back, yet he was soon writing songs that were surprisingly cosmopolitan.

In Rio, Djavan's unique musical style was at first no better received than in Maceió. While African music may have been "in his blood," as he says, his music in general was not characteristically *nordestino*—recognizably from northeastern Brazil—but instead reflected a broader background. Djavan was determined to address universal human concerns in his music, and he has clung to his vision of writing songs that everyone can relate to, regardless of their status or education. "The idea of different musical styles always interested me a lot," he says, "mixing this with that. Spanish music, Flamenco music, already interested me. African music I had in my blood. Luiz Gonzaga was also influential, as was Dorival Caymmi . . . My formation was very diverse, full of all kinds of information. The music I make today comes from exactly that mixture. But the most important music for me was African music, which in the northeast of Brazil is very significant."

Djavan refrained from composing political songs, such as those written by other MPB artists to protest the erosion of human rights after the 1963 Brazilian coup. He opted instead to build his reputation on songs about love. "I don't write protest songs," he once said. "I write love songs, and expressing love is a way of protesting against this violent world."

Djavan would seem an unlikely target for accusations of elitism. Yet the way in which he infuses his intonations of love with images from nature—the sun, sky, oceans, and stars—results in uniquely sophisticated lyrics. Like his eclectic music, his lyrics, though intended for everyone, were often considered unusual. "I have a way of saying things that is very personal, very private," he says. "It's not that people didn't understand my lyrics. They just found them different. People criticized them for being overly complex, elitist, and thought I was putting myself above others."

The artist attributes his lyrics' poetic quality in part to his wide reading of South American, Spanish, and Portuguese poets. "I've always liked poetry," he says. "I never had an advanced education, I never went to college, but I liked poetry. I've always worked with intuition, with sensibility. I read the great Brazilian poets—Carlos Drummond de Andrade, and a fantastic poet named Amelia Prado—Pablo Neruda from Chile, [Portuguese poet Fernando] Pessoa. I read Federico García Lorca all the time. It's really from there that [my inspiration] flows. My poetry comes very much from that kind of observation, from contemplation, which is something that's also really nordestino."

Djavan received his big break in 1975, when one of his songs, "Fato Consumado" (Consummated Fact), won second place at the Abertura Festival. The song became known all over Brazil and was responsible for launching his first album. In 1982, Djavan's third album, *Luz* (Light) was recorded in the United States with his band Sururu de Capote and guest musicians Stevie Wonder, Hubert Laws, and Ernie Watts. The lavishly produced, American-style recording was immensely popular in Brazil, where Djavan was fast becoming a superstar. His next release, *Lilás* (Lilac), also produced in the States, earned high praise from Quincy Jones and many other American musicians. Next, Djavan would return to his Brazilian roots, seeking a more authentically Brazilian sound with the album *Meu Lado* (My Side) in 1986.

I am an independent man. I've worked my whole life to be able to do what I want to do, at the moment that I want to do it, in whatever way I can. Everyone wants to have this kind of independence.

In 1989, he recorded an album for Columbia called, simply, *Djavan*. I love that recording—the Brazilian version, that is. Urged by his label to translate the Brazilian album from his native Portuguese into English and Spanish, Djavan sang in English for the U.S. version. I never felt that the American version worked, and when I asked him about it, he agreed. "I'm really someone else when I sing in another language," he conceded. "I'm just half of myself—sixty percent, at most."

He has since decided to avoid translations in the future. "I exploit the sound of the [Portuguese] language," he says. "There's a sonority to the words apart from the meaning, a sonority that has to be in sync with the music. I am a composer in Portuguese. My real objective is to show the beauty of my language to the world."

Djavan is the first to admit that the success of Brazilian music abroad is restricted in part because of the language barrier. Despite the tendency of the American and European recording industries to latch onto phenomena like *lambada*—used most appropriately, perhaps, in its early appearance in a European Orangina commercial—much of the best Brazilian music is seldom available outside of the country.

"I see it like this," Djavan concludes. "Brazilian music has a place in the world today as a music that's interesting and refined; a music that has a refined melody, a refined harmony, and a rhythmic richness and complexity. But it's a music that suffers, on the level of the international market, from an impasse due to language. If we spoke English in Brazil, I believe that Brazilian music would be the most popular in the world!"

When he contemplates his own evolution, from the penniless musician who stepped off of the bus in Rio to the international success he has become, Djavan is most thankful for having remained faithful to his own musical vision. "What makes me most proud," he says, "is being an independent human being. I'm not talking just about my career, but about my life. I am an independent man. I've worked my whole life to be able to do what I want to do, at the moment that I want to do it, in whatever way I can. Everyone wants to have this kind of independence. The successful man is the man who has a profession that he really enjoys, that he is a master of, that he does in his own way. That's not to say that he's totalitarian, that he doesn't listen, or that he's an egoist. No, this is a person who realizes himself by doing the things that he conceives in his mind. When I do a record, I'm committed only to my own personal satisfaction. I think that this is the great victory of my life."

Brian Eno

I first heard Brian Eno's music on *Music for Airports*, a groundbreaking recording that began as an installation of ethereal sounds and images at New York's La Guardia Airport in 1975. The music was unusual—soaring voices against a backdrop of dense synthesizer chords—yet none of it sounded artificial. Eno's subsequent *Ambient* series of the 1980s has influenced scores of artists on the trip-hop and ambient dub scenes, and he is a father figure to top producers like Michael Brook, Daniel Lanois, and Don Was, among many others. We've all heard music that has been influenced by his philosophy and by his unique producing style.

A natural eclectic and a true innovator, Eno is also an arresting theorist. His lectures illuminate ideas about music most of us never even consider. He is particularly fascinated by the way sound can create a completely original atmosphere. His remix of Massive Attack's "Protection" begins with the sound of rain, implying the theme of shelter and protection before the words begin.

Eno was among the first producers to conceive of the recording studio as an instrument. "I got involved with music," he says, "because an instrument came into existence—the

My feeling now is that music is aspiring to be like painting. I've always wanted to make music that was like painting in the sense of it being textural, physical in the way a painting is, nonnarrative in the way a painting is. I want to make music that is more like an Abstract Expressionist picture.

recording studio. And one of the reasons I succeeded was that not many people had thought of using it as an instrument, had thought that this might be a way of making music rather than transmitting music." As a producer—for U2 and many of the great albums on his own label, Opal, and Editions E.G.—he developed techniques that have changed the way pop records are made. He remains one of the industry's most sought-after producers.

In a lecture at the Los Angeles County Museum of Art, Eno said that he was initially inspired by "MOR" music—middle-of-the-road music of the 1950s and 1960s. He cited two influences in particular that I never would have associated with his work: the Ray Conniff Singers, and a song called "The Mountains High" by Dick and Dee Dee. "What attracted me most about this music," he says, "was the texture of it, the kind of acoustic landscape that recorded music could create. I mean, I knew orchestral music, and I knew jazz to some extent, but the excitement of rock music to me—popular recorded music if you like, which included the Ray Conniff Singers because they were very much a product of the recording studio—was a strangeness to the sound, a completely invented sense of place. 'The Mountains High' has an acoustic that couldn't have existed before the recording studio. And I think I was more interested in sonic quality than anything else."

In describing how music sounds, Eno often talks more like an architect or a geologist, or even a weather person. He once described his record *On Land* in terms of temperature, humidity, light, hardness and softness, texture and color. "Sometimes you hear things that are very cold or very warm," he explains. "I think a lot of people would use that phrase. I just wanted to extend that range of possibilities to include more specific landscape terms. Moist, dry—dry seems to me a very musical concept. I can imagine a dry sound as opposed to a moist one. I can imagine a liquid sound as opposed to a rock-like or mineral sound. And I've been thinking more and more over the last fifteen years or so that the type of language that one used to describe music—the classical language for describing music—is completely inadequate. Most of us are working with a much more extended sound palette than was available to classical composers. It has become important, I think, to try to find new ways of talking about sound. Just because it comes in through the ears, we still use the word music. But I think that what we're doing now is as different from classical music as, say, cinema is from classical painting. This is really a different art form."

With the exception of his adaptation of the Pachelbel Canon on his album *Discreet Music* (1975), Eno seems to have always been more interested in the possibilities inherent in pop than in those of classical music. But jazz, folk, and the blues have also been important sources for him. "I've always enjoyed folk music for its traditionalism," he says. "Blues, of course, I like very much, and gospel music, the close relative of blues. I like jazz more and more lately, because it reminds me of human beings, whereas a lot of the music I'm hearing now reminds me of computers, which I've gotten a little bit tired of. I was very much a proponent of computer music, and I think I was, as far as I know, the first person to use a drum machine on a record. I was very much into that kind of mechanistic sound, and now I'm bored with it. Jazz strikes me now particularly because I feel the frailty of the music, the possibility that it might all fall apart at any moment. There's a kind of act of faith involved in keeping it together."

I wondered if Eno thought that computer technology and sampling had irrevocably changed how pop music sounds, or if there might be a movement back to real instruments. "Well," he said, "all these technologies can be liberating, but they usually aren't. For instance, the sampler enables you to make any recorded sound into a musical instrument. Unfortunately, what people nearly always do with samplers is try to make string sounds or brass sounds, and in so doing they take away the most interesting thing about classical instruments, which is not that they have a particular sound, but that they have an intelligence playing them."

Eno brings this same outlook to his role as a producer. "My ability as a producer," he says, "lies in being enthusiastic about what people do. One of the biggest favors you can do for someone in a contemporary recording environment is to say, 'It's fine. It's really good in fact. Why don't you do something with it, just as it is?' Contemporary recording offers endless options for wasting time and for diffusing clarity. I've seen so many records ground into the dust by countless layers of overdubs and by experiments with every possible way of mixing the song until finally all enthusiasm and feeling for the thing has been lost. What's really impressive about a lot of old R & B records is that nothing is happening in them. There's a simple drum pattern, a bass sound, a guitar, and a voice, and passages in which nothing in particular is going on. The instruments are carrying on as they were before, and the guy has stopped singing, and there's kind of a nice hole there. And, you think, 'Ah, that sounds lovely. Yes, you can hear what those people are playing.'"

The late composer John Cage greatly influenced Eno's thinking. "I think without Cage I never would have become involved in music," he says. "Only Cage and a few other composers—Christian Wolfe, Cornelius Cardieu—were writing music for people with any level of competence. I began with a low level of competence. And here was the first music that invited me to perform it. Cage's music sent a message to the world that one could be a composer in the same way that one could be a painter and with the same kind of thoughts in mind—that there was a conceptual unity of the arts, between the arts, which have less to do with particular sets of tools and techniques than with approaches and ways of thinking. And though I don't completely follow the Cageian line here, those ideas allowed me to think that I might be able to make music, and because of him I started collecting tape recorders. The area I had some ideas about and where I assumed it would not be too hard to acquire competence was tape recording. I never tried to learn the guitar or anything like that."

Once, discussing landscape painting, Eno said that the way we look at a painting changes when a human figure is present. In a sense, that relates to ambient music and the way music is experienced and enjoyed. "Humans are naturally interested in other humans," he says. "If you make a painting with a human in it, no matter what scale that human is, you'll find that the eye constantly returns to that as the point of reference. Similarly, with music, if there is a voice it almost always becomes the center of our attention. I've found this extremely irksome, so I've deliberately either left the voice out, which is why I've made such a lot of instrumental music, or I've altered the voice in some way or another. I've used voices speaking different languages, made the voice strange enough sonically for it to become instrumental, and deliberately sung what could not possibly be construed as anything other than nonsense, so that people stop trying to find out what it means. That's the worst game to be playing when you're listening to music, I think—to be asking yourself, 'What does this mean?'"

Most of us have heard this quote from the nineteenth-century English art critic Walter Pater: "All art aspires to the condition of music." Eno doesn't agree. "I think when Pater said that, it was probably true," he explains. "He said that at a time when artists were moving away from the figurative in search of the abstract. They were trying to see whether it was possible to make paintings that didn't depend on being referential to other things in the world. Well, for the best part of a century people have been proving that that is possible, and my feeling now is that music is aspiring to be like painting. I've always wanted to make music that was like painting in the sense of being textural, physical in the way a painting is, nonnarrative in the way a painting is. I want to make music that is more like an Abstract Expressionist picture or a kind of experience that you immerse yourself in, not a story that you have to sit and listen to. One thing that's interesting about listening to music from around the world is that a lot of it sounds like rubbish if you don't share the same cultural assumptions. For instance, if you listen to Thai classical music, the first thing you think is, 'This is all out of tune.' Well, they have a different musical scale. They don't divide up the frequency spectrum the way we do. And it's hard to listen to. So, music is very culturally conditioned, I think. There's no sense in which it's some unified field of emotional activity that we all participate in. We happen to belong to the most powerful music form in the world. Western pop music is very dominant at the moment, so we might be tempted to think that all music will communicate with everyone just because we've been able to propagandize ours for so long and so well."

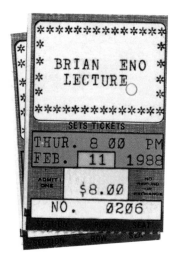

Asha Bhosle & Lata Mangeshkar

Not long ago in a Santa Monica gas station I heard the unmistakable voice of Lata Mangeshkar pouring out of the loudspeaker. When I mentioned this to the attendant, he looked at me incredulously. "You know the Divine Lata? How do you know our Lata?" he asked, claiming her with an obvious sense of national pride. Although little-known outside of India or perhaps London, Lata Mangeshkar and Asha Bhosle are the world's most recorded singers. Their voices, high-pitched and childlike, have been used in thousands of *ghazals*, the ubiquitous love songs featured in the dozens of melodramas turned out annually by Bollywood, as the Bombay film industry is known. For thirty years, the two women have sung of ecstasy and heartbreak to millions. They are known as "playback singers," singers whose voices are dubbed over the voices of actors in Indian films. First they record the song used in the film; then the actors listen to the playback and mime the words before the cameras. In this way, they exert an invisible yet constant presence in the films.

Lata Mangeshkar and Asha Bhosle happen to be sisters. Lata, the older of the pair, was born in 1928, and has ap-

peared in the *Guinness Book of Records* as the World's Most Recorded Artist, with over 30,000 songs recorded in more than 2,000 films. Asha isn't far behind. Together they specialize in sentimental *ghazals*, a song form brought to India centuries ago by the Persians, as well as in a newer form that began about thirty years ago, the faster songs used in *masala*, or "spice" films. The two women exercise a vocal hegemony in Indian films and soundtracks and are unlikely to be unseated. After so many years of welcome familiarity, the vast Indian public may not believe what they see on the silver screen if they don't hear the voices of these two everpopular vocalists.

Beny Moré

A legend of Latin music, Beny Moré was the most important Cuban singer and bandleader in the 1950s, rivaled in popularity and influence only by Celia Cruz. Although his career was cut short by an early death, Moré left an impressive number of great recordings, most accomplished with his sensational Banda Gigante. Recording for RCA, the group featured a classic big band lineup, but with a Cuban rhythm section adding fire and vitality. In front of this propulsive machine was one of the greatest voices ever to come out of Cuba. No one who listens to Moré's stunning "Que Buena Baila Usted" (How Well You Dance) can fail to be converted by the intensity and power of his music.

Known as "El Barbaro del Ritmo" (Barbarian of Rhythm), Beny Moré was born in Santa Isabel de las Lajas, Cuba, in 1919. He began his career by bringing his guitar to parties, and became well

known in his hometown before moving to Havana in 1940, where he played first in cafés and parks, and then in clubs. He migrated to Mexico City and sang with Perez Prado, rising in popularity with the emergence of the mambo. In the early 1950s, with bandleader Rafael de Paz, he recorded the great Afro-Cuban song "Yiri Yiri Bon," which became a huge hit.

Moré's greatest work came after he formed Banda Gigante in Havana in 1953. With the band he performed and recorded classic big band numbers, mambos, *sons*, chachachas, and slow, unforgettable boleros. Hip New Yorkers in the late 1940s knew Cuban music through bands like those of Miguelito Valdes and Machito, who helped to create the Cuban bebop, or "Cubop," style with Charlie Parker and Dizzy Gillespie. Cuban music was also popularized in the U.S. by the radio broadcasts of Perez Prado and Xavier Cugat. Beny Moré, however, took Cuban music to a new level. His voice, belied by his reputation as the Barbarian of Rhythm, was suave and passionate. His big band was one of the most galvanizing swing organizations ever recorded.

Privately, Moré was wild and unpredictable. His failure to turn up for gigs cost him many jobs. He was admired by some for his fearless, sometimes brazen attitude, but he also went too far and alienated many people. In Venezuela, he once wrapped a newspaper around a lead pipe and nearly beat to death a promoter who hadn't paid him, an act for which he spent time in jail.

Moré lived impulsively and destructively, and died in 1963 of cirrhosis of the liver at the age of 43; but as a musician, he earned his place in Latin music's pantheon of mambo kings. His legacy can still be felt on the Latin music scene and wherever people look for great tropical sounds. A steady flow of CD reissues and a constant presence on radio airwaves has ensured that Moré's music will not be forgotten.

Cesaria Evora

Cesaria Evora was one of the great discoveries of international music in 1992. She had been singing for most of her life on the small, desolate islands of the Cape Verde archipelago, three hundred miles off the coast of Senegal. Considered the queen of *morna*, the best-known of several traditional Cape Verdean musical styles, Evora has a rich, smoky voice that recalls Nina Simone, and a smooth legato delivery reminiscent of Billie Holiday.

Like the blues, morna (which derives from the English, "to mourn") is a traditional expression of both deep sorrow and love. When you first hear morna—which is to Cape Verde what *fado* is to Portugal or the tango to Argentina—you hear something of the music of Brazil, Portugal, and Africa, yet it doesn't really sound like any of these. Dating back to at least the early nineteenth century, it is a style unique to these small islands. "Only [morna]," Evora has said, "can calm our pain and make us forget our difficulties, our sadness released."

Discovered in the fifteenth century by Portuguese sailors, who used it as a way station during voyages down the coast of West Africa, the drought-plagued and rugged Cape Verde archipelago has been independent since 1975. Evora grew

I used to sing for a lot of tourists, and they liked it. I always thought there was a chance that I could be an artist one day. I felt that once I took my music outside of Cabo Verde, strangers would like it, and that is exactly what happened.

up with her mother and grandmother in Mindelo, a small town on the island of São Vicente. Like many Cape Verdeans, her father left the islands in search of work; she was only seven years old. Despite the harsh realities of poverty and emigration—some two thirds of a million Cape Verdeans live abroad, mainly in Europe and the U.S.—Evora describes her childhood as positive. "The island is poor, but it's full of sun, music, and fish," she says. "I had a good upbringing. We are not a sad people, because we live out of hope—we hope that one day it will rain."

Even as a young girl Evora knew that she had a beautiful voice. "When I was little," she explains, "I would sit on my father's lap and sing children's songs. Later, when I turned sixteen, a man discovered me and told me that I had a beautiful voice. From then on, I continued singing. My mother didn't know that I went out to sing at those little clubs and cabarets, because I was too young. But when she found out, she was happy."

During the '60s, '70s, and much of the '80s, Evora sang in small bars for Mindelo tourists and regulars who gave her change for food and drinks. "Sometimes I would sing in bars," she recalls, "and other times in private homes for parties and other social functions. Morna music was originally sung at funeral processions. Whenever visitors came to Cabo Verde, they would ask me to sing." In the 1960s, Evora made a few radio recordings,

but they never led to contracts. "When my music was played on the radio, everybody in Cabo Verde knew it was me!" she says. "The radio station still has those early tapes, and still plays them from time to time."

In 1987, while traveling through Portugal with a women's group, Evora was discovered by entrepreneur José de Silva while singing in a restaurant. A Cape Verdean, de Silva arranged for several of her subsequent recordings on his own label, Lusafrica. French radio began to play her music, and public response was ecstatic. "Sodade," perhaps her most popular single, was a hit in France in 1993, and the LP it came from, *Miss Perfumado*, sold 350,000 copies worldwide. That same year, she performed a standing-room-only concert at the famed Olympia Theatre, where divas like Edith Piaf and Portuguese fado queen Amália Rodrigues had made their Parisian debuts. "My fame was born in France," she told me. Her American debut came in 1994, followed by a best-selling release on Nonesuch Records in 1995.

During the long years in Mindelo, Evora held to the conviction that one day her music might have meaning for others outside of her country. "I used to sing for a lot of tourists, and they liked it," she said. "I always thought there was a chance that I could be an artist one day. I felt that once I took my music outside of Cabo Verde, strangers would like it, and that is exactly what happened. Being as

old as I am, I never expected to be so well accepted, and I am very happy about that."

Evora has a famously nonchalant presence onstage. She sometimes sits down at a small table to take a cigarette break and, formerly—she no longer drinks—a sip of brandy. "I have always done this," she said, "since the beginning. Wherever I perform, whether in bars or at private parties, I always take a smoke break." Her most famous trademark, however, is her penchant for stepping onstage barefoot. "*La Diva Aux Pieds Nus* was the title of my first album in France," she explains. "They called it that because I don't like shoes. I traveled with four or five pairs of shoes, but they always stayed in the luggage. I like my feet to feel at ease. I always walk barefoot in Cabo Verde. The ground is hot there."

I asked Evora about the word *sodade* (from the Portuguese *saudade*), which comes up repeatedly in her songs, as well as in Brazilian and Portuguese music. "Sodade is sodade!" she said. "It is part of our music, but it exists everywhere. It's what we feel when a certain person is on a trip or leaves. Fishermen leave, people who finish school go from Cape Verde to find work. People go to Holland to work on ships. There's a lot of emigration from Cape Verde. People separate and miss each other. That's one reason there's so much sodade."

Emigration exists everywhere, of course, but it is an especially salient reality in Cape Verde. Evora experienced it firsthand with her father's departure, and nearly all Cape Verdeans have relatives abroad. One of her songs, "My Fatigue is Endless," captures the heartache of constant emigration perfectly. It talks about workers who leave their families behind in Cape Verde to find work in São Tomé, a small island off the coast of Gabon. They return, only to leave again.

Since her arrival on the international music scene, Evora has on occasion said that she regrets it took so long for her to find success. I wanted to know how it has affected her life. "Outside of Cabo Verde, I make a good living," she says. "My concerts and albums are selling well, thank God. Having financial means allows me to travel, buy a home, have a few luxuries, and live an easier life. But my life in Mindelo goes on pretty much the same, except I have more money. My feelings about life haven't changed, however. I am the same person."

Evora has a fondness for other female singers who, like her, have lived the hard lives described in their songs. "I don't vary the music much, because I have my favorites," she said when I asked her what she listens to at home. "I put on Billie Holiday, Amália Rodrigues, and that French girl, Edith Piaf."

The last time I had seen Evora in the studio, she said she would never again live with a man. Abandoned by three husbands, she'd finally had enough. I reminded her of this. "That's true," she said. But I had since heard that romance had again entered her life. "I have many or none," she sighed. "It's feast or famine. All kidding aside, I live with my mom, my children, and my two grandchildren. I have no man in my life. Perhaps a man will fall out of the heavens, but so far I haven't seen any."

Antonio Carlos Jobim

When we think of Brazilian music, we quickly get to the name of the late Antonio Carlos "Tom" Jobim. I always knew his work, but it took years for me to appreciate just how great a composer he was. I am not alone in believing that he is one of the great twentieth-century composers and one of the finest composers of all time. He wrote beautiful and deceptively simple melodies over complex yet fluid harmonic arrangements, enriched with a sense of humor and appreciation of life's small pleasures (and shared sadnesses). As much as in Mozart, an essential humanism illuminates all of Jobim's music.

Few people outside of Brazil had heard much Brazilian music before the first wave of bossa nova songs swept America and Europe in the 1960s, introduced by Stan Getz and sung so lyrically by João Gilberto. As developed by Jobim, Gilberto, and Vinícius De Moraes, bossa nova displayed a finesse and sophistication, influenced by modern jazz and European classical music, previously unheard in Brazilian music. It took Brazilians a while to love this new style, so far removed from samba and popular music of the late 1950s.

Jobim's melodies have a timeless quality, and, like the music of Bach, a compelling logic and perfection that brings musicians and singers back to them again and again. "The Girl from Ipanema," to cite one example, is among the most popular songs of the last thirty years. Frank Sinatra brought Jobim to New York to record an album, *Sinatra & Company* (Reprise Records, 1969), and his music has been covered by countless artists, from pop bands to symphony orchestras. Jobim was not a great singer or pianist; his legacy resides in the genius of his compositions.

Antonio Carlos Jobim was born in 1927 in a middle-class Rio de Janeiro neighborhood called Tijuca. He grew up in the Rio ambience of sun, sea, and soccer, and loved the abundant natural wonders of Rio, which in his youth was still relatively pristine and unpolluted. He studied with a piano teacher from Berlin who advocated serialist music. Jobim learned a great deal of harmony and theory from him, but never turned his back on the popular music of Brazil. Like many jazz modernists, Jobim was influenced by the music of Ravel and Debussy, but once remarked that they "didn't have this African beat that we have here."

In his early twenties, Jobim began performing in Rio nightclubs, and hanging out with musicians such as Dorival Caymmi, flautist and composer Pixinguinha, and others. His talent as a songwriter didn't fully blossom, however, until he teamed up with the brilliant and fast-living diplomat-lyricist Vinícius De Moraes. De Moraes, a lawyer, poet, graduate of Oxford, and one-time Brazilian Vice Consul in Los Angeles, wrote the lyrics to most of the great Jobim songs, including "The Girl from Ipanema." There was a magic chemistry and a sense of fun between Jobim and De Moraes; together they created a cool, care-free new music that captured a typically Brazilian sensibility just as the country was slipping

riginal Words and Mus

NTONIO CARLOS JC

nglish Words by GENE

saw walking past their favorite beachfront hangout. I saw Jobim perform several times. Accompanied by a fine trombonist and cellist, he played piano, with his wife and daughters in the chorus. The harmonically rich textures created by the choral lines, trombone, and cello gave the music abundant lyricism. Only a romantic like Jobim would think of having solos and frontline melodies played by a cello and trombone—a touch of genius. In my view, Jobim deserves a place next to George Gershwin, Cole Porter, Lennon and McCartney, and other titans of twentieth-century popular music.

tragically into a long and bitter period of brutal dictatorship. Nevertheless, it was a captivating music that the world has celebrated ever since.

Stan Getz brought Jobim's music to America with his classic 1963 album *Getz/Gilberto*. The soft voice of João Gilberto found a lyrical complement in Getz's lithe playing style, as did the dry, almost monotone vocal delivery of Astrud Gilberto on "The Girl from Ipanema," a song inspired by a woman Jobim and Vinícius often

Djivan Gasparyan

Djivan Gasparyan makes some of the most arresting and soulful music I've ever heard. It starts with the plaintive, haunting sound of the traditional Armenian duduk, a cylindrical wooden flute of which he is the undisputed master. The Armenian American writer William Saroyan called the sound the duduk produces—a rich, reedy, and resonant tone, its clear lines of mesmerizing melody punctuated by the whisper of breath—the sound of prayer. And it is a very old prayer, emanating from a long history filled with suffering.

I first heard Gasparyan's recording *I Will Not Be Sad in this World* in 1989, after Brian Eno brought it to the attention of the world. He had first heard it at a friend's home in Moscow around the time of the devastating 1988 earthquake in Armenia and was immediately transfixed. It is music filled with pathos and longing, a music with strong connections to ancient church and folk traditions and to the religious identity of the Armenian people. It has a synaesthetic quality that evokes a rich tapestry of images; it's been used to great effect in such films as *The Last Temptation of Christ* and *Dead Man Walking*.

Most of Gasparyan's music is based on old Armenian folk melodies. He plays long, caressing lines with a natural yet

We've had many happy moments, but the majority of our existence has been a life of oppression. That has definitely influenced our music. I too wonder, 'Why is our music so sad?' But that's how we are . . . Armenian people are born into sadness.

carefully modulated vibrato; his phrases are gentle and sustained, punctuated only by his careful breathing. More than anything else, this plaintive music is filled with the yearning and joys of the Armenian people.

Gasparyan is humble when talking about his music, yet he can be credited with rescuing the duduk from obscurity. Made of apricot wood, the duduk is a pipe with eight finger holes on the upper side and one on the reverse. Ethnomusicologists trace its history to A.D. 400, though some Armenian scholars insist that its beginnings date back as far as 1200 B.C. Like the bassoon and *ghaita*, the duduk is a double-reed instrument, producing a warm, soft sound somewhere between a flute and an oboe. Since it has only a one-octave range, its expressiveness is the result of careful embouchure, fingering technique, and nuanced phrasing. Gasparyan describes it in far more elegant terms: "The duduk has a soul and feelings in itself. It's the purified symphony of human spirits. In its tiny holes it bears the cry of Armenia's bitter past, and a hymn to the present—bright life, their faith, their righteousness, and their titanic strength. I have loved it since age eight. It was very commonly used when I was young, during the 1940s. I took it up and I bought several and started to perform in youth groups, which I stayed with until I became a professional."

Gasparyan was born in Solag, a small village on the outskirts of the present-day Armenian capital of Yerevan. At six he began to listen and learn from the old masters; he is otherwise self-taught. In 1948, he joined the Tatool Altounian National Song and Dance Ensemble and made his professional debut as a soloist with the Yerevan Philharmonic Orchestra. Since then, Gasparyan has been cited many times for his artistry. He has received Gold Medals at international competitions organized by UNESCO and is the only musician to receive the honorary title of People's Artist of Armenia from the Armenian government. Besides his solo efforts, he has recorded with the Kronos Quartet, the Los Angeles Philharmonic, and has performed at festivals throughout Europe, America, and Asia.

I Will Not Be Sad in this World was first recorded in 1983; it was licensed and released internationally (with a new title) after Eno discovered it. "They called me from Moscow and asked me to go there after they had discovered it," Gasparyan recalls. "From there we went to London. It was after the 1988 earthquake that the title was changed. One song already had the title, 'In this world I will not be sad and cry.' So we thought it would be good, after the earthquake, to use this title for the whole CD. The history of Armenians has been a tragic one." Gasparyan gave all the profits from the CD to the earthquake victims.

A song on another album, *Moon Shines at Night*, is titled "December 7, 1988," the date of the earthquake. He was in Yerevan at that time. "In Yerevan we didn't feel so much," he says. "There was no news, no word from the epicenter, Spitak. I had friends in Spitak, so I went there. There was no life left, the church bells had fallen, all the buildings were in ruins. For months all they did was recover dead bodies."

I asked him about the sad nature of his and, in fact, most Armenian music. "We've had many happy moments," he replied, "but the majority of our existence has been a life of oppression. That has definitely influenced our music. I too wonder, 'Why is our music so sad?' But that's how we are."

"It's not only the holocaust," he continued, referring to the massacre of some one and a half million Armenians at the hands of the Turks in 1915 and 1916. "But before then, long centuries ago, we had successive tragedies—massacres and invasions. Armenian people are born into sadness. And we have heard this music from our own fathers, and we love this music even though it is sad. That is what we have inherited, and that is what comes through in the performance of our music. We can't help it. But that doesn't mean that our music is only sad music. There are many happy occasions where we play the duduk. But even on those happy occasions, we play love songs and lyric songs which have a sad aspect to them."

Not long ago, I was returning from the Los Angeles Airport in a taxicab, and it happened that our driver was Armenian. My first question, of course, was, "Do you know the music of Djivan Gasparyan?" He was surprised that I knew of it. He started talking with great enthusiasm, and continued for some time. Gasparyan is very famous in Armenia and among Armenians all over the world. I asked Gasparyan if he could walk down the street in Armenia without being stopped by fans, and whether or not he had problems with privacy. "They know me from my appearances on TV," he said. "And they've heard me on radio and seen my pictures. Many who see me for the first time react very strongly; they do recognize me, and ask me, 'Is it you, Djivan?!' When I say yes, they don't know what to do or what to give to me. When I go to the market, they always want to give me their produce to take home."

In Armenia today, the duduk is again being taught in the schools. Gasparyan is proud that younger Armenians are once again eager to learn about and play the instrument and to celebrate their rich cultural heritage. "It is my great desire to pass on this beautiful tradition to my grandchildren and to all the young people. I have two grandchildren, and I have already started them on playing the duduk. I also teach many young people. It's very much loved by everybody. There's no concert or social occasion where the duduk is not played."

Salif Keita

Fusing traditional Manding melodies and rhythms—the music of the Mandinka people of Senegal and neighboring regions—with modern instruments and electronic technology, Malian musician Salif Keita has created a sound all his own.

In the early 1970s, Keita played traditional roots music with a group called the Rail Band, so named because they performed at the Buffet Hotel train station restaurant in Bamako, Mali. He then joined another group in Bamako, Les Ambassadeurs du Motel, which incorporated Latin, rock, and other pop sounds into its repertoire. Several albums later, and with the huge success of "Mandjou," Keita was on his way to international fame. Now living in Paris, the singer-composer continues to draw international audiences with his spellbinding performances and an otherworldly voice that has been described as haunting, primal, and searing.

The third of thirteen children, Keita was born in 1949 in a village west of Bamako called Djoliba. He is a descendent of Sunjata Keita, also known as Dulu Kharanayne or the African Alexander the Great, who in A.D. 1240 founded the Mandinka empire. This lineage placed him in the traditional ruling caste of Manding society, so when he decided to

sider. What he considers an unhappy childhood began at birth. Keita is albino. In his music, he describes his own inner turmoil—the challenge of accepting that you're different from everyone else—and his experience with an often insensitive world. "It was difficult for others to accept a white child coming from a black mother and black father," he explains. "They are very traditional and don't have any explanation for albinism." In fact, giant slabs of stone upon which albinos and other so-called "troublemakers" were once sacrificed still remain just outside his village.

Singing helped Keita to combat his feelings of loneliness. "When I was young," he says, "I would go out into the fields and shout and scream at the monkeys and birds. It was at that time that people told me I had a powerful voice. It was something that helped me fight against loneliness. . . . When I started to sing, I tried to exorcise my sufferings through my voice. It was to release the suffering."

become a musician Keita faced opposition from his family, in particular from his father. It was not considered respectable for someone of his noble status to sing for a living among the ranks of the musician caste, which included the wandering *griots* who performed for royal courts in precolonial times. The tension forced Keita to offer an ultimatum. "I asked him if he wanted to see me become a gangster or a musician," he recalls.

The conflict caused by Keita's musical ambition was one of many obstacles he faced while growing up that set him off as an out-

While his path toward musical success has been defined by struggle, it began almost accidentally. He originally wanted to teach, but poor eyesight kept him from that vocation. "I was in the street," he recalls, "and I visited the home of my elder brothers because I didn't want to go home. One of them had a guitar, which I took to work. That's how I learned, playing three or four songs and singing at the same time. I started to spend time in the bars of Bamako, making my living out of those four songs."

Even when he was approached to form an orchestra—a proposal that eventually led to a

> My only concern when I sing is the people who have come to see me—that they receive everything they have come for. Because to me, singing is like an exchange of energy, in both directions. The more I give, the more I get.

four-year stint with the Rail Band in the early '70s—he initially resisted. He still wasn't serious about music. "Singing was more like a hobby, a bridge before I got a job. Not a vocation really, but it was more [honest] to sing than to steal. So I stayed." It was only when he hooked up with Les Ambassadeurs and headed for the Ivory Coast that Keita realized his hobby was his true calling.

Keita talks freely about the music that has inspired him. His earliest influence was Cuban music, which has had a significant impact on West Africa. One of his favorite groups was the great Cuban *charanga* ensemble Orquesta Aragón. Many people believe that Manding music traveled to Cuba centuries ago with the slave trade, which explains certain similarities between Cuban and traditional Manding rhythms. It has come back to Mali in our own era, to be reinterpreted by artists like Keita. He also cites as early influences James Brown, Tina Turner, Pink Floyd, Spanish flamenco, and the Guinean singer Kouyate Sory Kandia.

Keita's own fame is not something he takes lightly. "I feel like a missionary," he explains, "or rather, a messenger who speaks for the whole universe—to those who are interested in my music and who try to understand my ideas." It's a relationship he describes as "completely spiritual," and is opposed to politics, which does not interest him. "Politics is not real, it is abstract," he says. "It is a lie, politics."

Keita has become famous for his prayerlike gestures when he walks on stage. "My only concern when I sing," he told the *Los Angeles Times*, "is the people who have come to see me—that they receive everything they have come for. Because to me, singing is like an exchange of energy, in both directions. The more I give, the more I get."

Having achieved the international success he desired, Keita hasn't forgotten his roots. Reflections on the past and thoughts about his Malian heritage are always close at hand. Lyrics from his most recent album, *Folon* (*The Past*), reveal just how near they are.

> *In the Past, we simply took orders*
> *even though you thought about happiness*
> *even if you were intelligent*
> *you could not express yourself*
> *now, no one can decide for us.*

Andrés Segovia

Only a great artist can take a little-known music and make it world class. Piazzolla did it with the tango, Ravi Shankar did it with classical Indian music, and Andrés Segovia did it with Spanish guitar music. He made the guitar a respected concert instrument, toured the world well into his eighties, and performed and recorded many works written for him by Castelnuovo-Tedesco, Ponce, and other composers. He also dedicated himself to the herculean task of transcribing many classical works written for the piano, including a great deal of Bach, for the guitar.

Segovia was born in Linares, Spain, in 1893. He gave debut recitals in Granada in 1909, Madrid in 1912, and Paris in 1924. Beginning in the 1960s, I saw him perform whenever I could. Every four years or so he came to Los Angeles, and each time he seemed to walk on stage a little more frail than the time before. The last time I saw him, he walked with a cane, assisted by a colleague, and another assistant brought his guitar once he was seated. The second he entered the stage, the crowd gave him a rousing and reverential ovation. We all knew this might be the last time we would see him perform. And indeed it was. Segovia died in 1987, in Madrid, at the age of ninety-four.

Today great guitarists, such as the Assad Brothers from Brazil, the Romeros, Christopher Parkening, and Cuba's Manuel Barrueco, continue to record, perform internationally, and earn their livelihood by playing classical works composed for or transcribed for guitar. Segovia made it possible.

Camarón de la Isla

Camarón de la Isla was adored by millions of all ages during his short lifetime. When he died in July 1992 of lung cancer at age 41, Spanish television programs were interrupted, musicians cancelled concerts, and the mayor of Barcelona ordered three days of official public mourning. Madrid's leading daily newspaper, *El País*, devoted four pages to the late singer. Spanish music critics declared that flamenco had been orphaned, and no singer has emerged to continue Camarón's legacy.

Born in 1950 to a poor family on the island of San Fernando, near Cádiz in southwest Spain, Jose Monge Cruz was nicknamed "Camarón de la Isla" (Shrimp of the Island) by an uncle because of his slender build and because his skin, as white as the famous large shrimp of Cádiz, was pale for a gypsy. He was the youngest of eight children, and his father, like many gypsies in the past, was a blacksmith. While working in his father's shop, Camarón sang work songs, called *martinetes*, a cappella to the rhythm of the hammer striking the anvil. He dreamed of becoming a bullfighter, but showed an early gift for singing.

Camarón first won acclaim at the age of twelve at the Montilla amateur flamenco festival. Real fame was sparked several years later by an appearance at the Dolores Vargas club, where the specialty was the explosive *cante jondo* (deep song), a traditional form of gypsy singing and the most powerful of flamenco styles. Camarón was shy, however, and he was unsettled by the publicity his talent provoked, a situation that eventually led him to escape into alcohol and drugs.

In the 1970s, Camarón experimented with many musical styles. Conservatives at first attacked him for taking liberties with traditional forms, but critics eventually admitted that he was exceptional. By the age of twenty-six, he was universally recognized as the greatest flamenco singer in Spain.

Camarón sang with what the Spanish call *duende*—unbelievable intensity and profound depth. His haunting and pain-filled voice also had a violent, corrosive edge known as *rajo*, a flamenco term that means "searing." His phrasing was immaculate, and he amazed audiences with his gift for matching the cadences of the *palmas* (precision clapping). He mastered all of the traditional flamenco styles, and brought flamenco out of the conservative milieu of the Franco years, capturing young audiences in the newly democratic Spain of the 1980s.

Camarón de la Isla lived intensely. His final album, *Potro de Rabia y Miel* (Little Colt of Rage and Honey), recorded early in 1992 with Paco de Lucia and Tomatito, is devastating listening. It reminds me of Billie Holiday's last recording, *Lady in Satin*, or Jacques Brel's *Les Marquises*. In the voice of each you hear a ravaged, unforgettable final cry: of rage, of anguish, of despair.

Khaled

Khaled, the "King of Rai," is the most popular singer among young people in the Arab world. Despite—or because of—the stranglehold Islamic fundamentalists have on Algeria, he has sold millions of records and emerged as a voice of individual freedom and human rights.

Khaled Hadj Brahim was born in Sidi-El-Houari, near the port city of Oran, in 1960, during the height of Algeria's bloody war of independence. "They call Oran the 'Little Paris' of Algeria," Khaled told me. "It's really the only city in Algeria where there are a lot of people moving around and artists coming in, and where there is a lot of life and creativity."

Khaled's first musical influences were the great Egyptian singers Umm Kulthum and Farid el-Atrache, as well as French singers Edith Piaf and Charles Aznavour. I asked him about other inspirations. "I grew up listening to Johnny Halliday and Elvis Presley," he said. "I started with music pretty young, playing different types of instruments like harmonica, guitar, and flute. The best time to do it was at weddings. There were a lot of influences coming into Oran, mostly from France, which was tied up very strongly with Algeria, but also from the U.S. We imitated Elvis Presley a lot."

They called me the devil, and my music the devil's music. It's like the rock and roll story in America. Eventually people get used to it and start enjoying it.

Sometimes referred to as the "North African blues," *rai* began as a music for the common person, free from classical trappings or elitism. I asked Khaled to define rai. "The word rai means opinion, as in your opinion, your ideology. Rai music started at weddings, where men and women were separated. The women would gather together, singing, talking, and saying things about the men that they couldn't otherwise say in mixed company. *Ya rai* means something akin to 'tell it like it is.'"

Until the 1940s, rai was always performed privately because the lyrics were too brazen to be sung in public. Then, it entered the cabarets in Oran. Women were the style's first artists. Among the young urban and illiterate rural poor of Algeria, they had the lowest status, and polite society turned its back on women who sang and danced. Early rai singers like Cheikha Remitti, known as the "Piaf of rai," were considered outcasts. Pop began to be integrated into rai in the late 1960s, and by the 1970s singers like Khaled went even further, updating rai by combining a traditional Islamic singing style with Moroccan and Egyptian pop, Spanish flamenco, soul, reggae—basically whatever came into the country after it was liberated from the French in 1962.

Khaled made his first record, a single called "The Road to School," while still a student. Like most rai artists, he first appeared under the name "Cheb," which means "youthful" or "attractive." It was used to denote an artist of the new and rebellious generation, rather than from the old, classical order. The early 1980s found him in Marseilles, performing his music in cafés, an insouciant, carefree singer gaining an increasingly large following. Khaled put a dance groove into rai, using synthesizers and drum machines, and soon became its most popular artist. His lyrics sometimes speak of human rights and liberation from traditional mores; at other times, like rock and roll, they're just about having a good time.

"In France or the U.S., people who don't understand a word of what you're singing still get into the groove and love it," Khaled says. "There is something in the blood, a feeling you get through the music that doesn't really have to be understood in the lyrics. When I was a kid and I was listening to songs in English, I didn't understand them. It worked for me, and I guess it does the same for them."

Khaled now lives in Paris, where he is extremely popular. "This music existed for centuries," he says of his work, "but someone had to get out of Oran and promote it. Paris was a first step." Politically, it has sometimes been difficult for him in France, since right-wing factions in and outside of Algeria have taken public exception to his music and what they believe it represents. There was also the language barrier. "Initially," he told me, "top-forty radio wouldn't play my music—they wouldn't go for it because it was sung in Arabic. Usually you have to sing in French to be accepted at those stations. But it started getting airplay anyway, and it crossed over, Arabic lyrics and all." Khaled's "Didi" was, in fact, the first Arabic-language song to break into the top ten on the French charts. The single is from his 1992 album *Khaled*. Its producer, Don Was, gave Khaled a smoother sound and allowed him to engage an even wider audience.

Khaled's sensual love songs challenge traditional ideas about women as possessions. This has made him a target of Islamic militants, who believe that singing about sex is immoral. "In Algeria," he told one interviewer, "it has been forbidden to sing about women. In all the classical songs, women are usually represented by gazelles or other metaphors. I go further, and sing about real love between a man and a woman. It's more direct than the traditional music." Religious extremists have also been provoked by images in Khaled's videos, which have shown him with a glass of wine (forbidden by Islam), surrounded by women. "People have accused me of writing songs about drinking and sex," he said. "If I sing about drinking, it's like this: I have a song about a guy ordering a drink, and the bartender asks him why he's drinking. The guy tells him he's drinking because he's trying to forget about a woman who has left him. So the song is about love, not alcohol."

The danger Khaled lives with is very real. Several Algerian artists, including the producer Rachid Baba-Ahmed, singer Cheb Hasni, and recently the popular Berber singer Lounès Matoub, have been murdered by religious fundamentalists. In the past, too, Khaled has lived in France with a woman not his wife. "When someone does that in Algeria, it's a catastrophe before the parents' (and everybody else's) eyes," he once observed. "Rai speaks about that mentality—can't do this, can't do that, this sin, that sin . . . I'm a real believer, even too much of a believer, but one mustn't condemn someone to death for having fun. I've studied the Koran, and as far as I'm concerned he who wants to pray has his mosque in front of him, and he who wants to have fun goes his own way and that's all there is to it."

Fundamentalists believe Khaled sings the devil's music. "They called me the devil," he says, "and my music the devil's music. It's like the rock and roll story in America. Eventually people get used to it and start enjoying it." His 1993 song "N'ssi N'ssi," a huge hit in France, went to the top of the charts in Egypt before it was banned there. The authorities didn't understand the lyrics; they only knew that Khaled was a bad boy, so his lyrics must be subversive. This recalls the controversy over the '50s song "Louie Louie," by Richard Berry. No one understood the lyrics—they are indecipherable—but the song was banned anyway; people thought it was about sex. In fact, Khaled's music is pure groove; it celebrates life. But it celebrates life in a dangerous time, in places where personal liberty is restricted. So Khaled, despite his fame, is forced to walk a tightrope, and his life is under constant threat.

Nusrat Fateh Ali Kahn

The late Nusrat Fateh Ali Khan was the king of *qawwals*, Pakistani Sufi singers who embrace music as a form of devotion, a way of achieving transcendence and drawing nearer to the divine. *Qawwali*, which means "wise or philosophical utterance," is a vocal expression of Sufism, the mystical sect of Islam. In Pakistan and in countries with large Pakistani communities, Nusrat was a superstar. His fans danced, whirled, shouted, and hurled crumpled, large-denomination bank notes at him as a sign of appreciation and respect. His concerts featured traditional devotional music, and he swept the audiences into a frenzy. His music has a rapturous, otherworldly quality that transcends language and enters the heart as pure feeling.

Nusrat's music was first championed in the West by Peter Gabriel, who recorded him as part of a live World of Music Arts and Dance (WOMAD) festival in 1983. I remember listening to the five-minute excerpt of Nusrat's WOMAD performance on the 1984 double LP *Music and Rhythm*. It was unlike anything I had ever heard. His singing communicated tremendous emotion with a breathtaking urgency and virtuosity. Four years passed before his first solo recording was

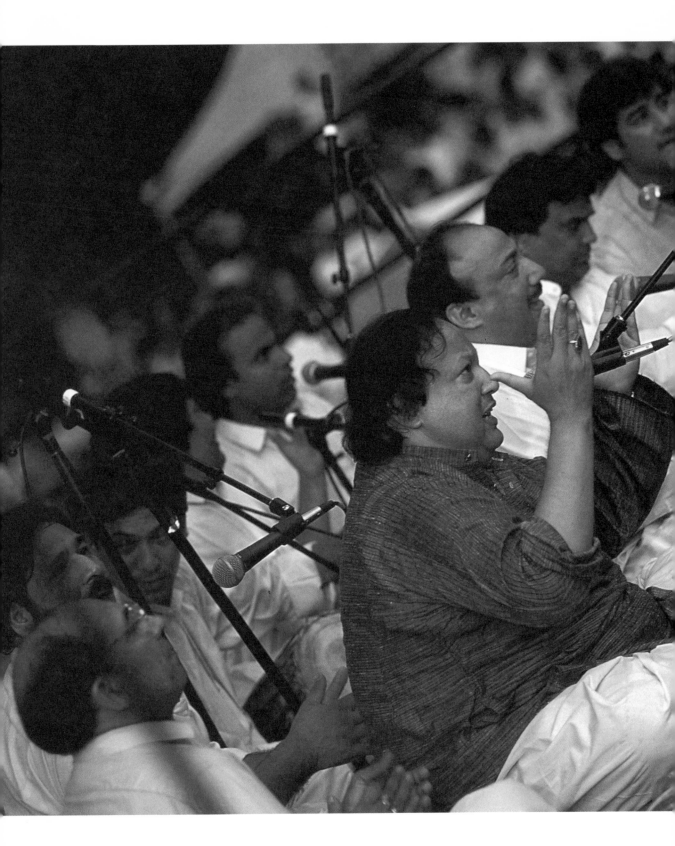

released in the U.S. Later came Massive Attack's remix of "Mustt Mustt" (A Man and His Work), and his success in Europe, America, and around the world was assured.

Nusrat Fateh Ali Khan was born on October 13, 1948, in Lyallpur (now Faisalabad), in the Punjab region of Pakistan, heir to a Khan family dynasty of qawwali singers and classical musicians that goes back six hundred years. His parents wanted him to become a doctor, but the young boy was so inspired by his father's voice that he, too, decided to sing. He first sang in public at his father's funeral in 1964, after which he became a qawwal following a premonitory dream. "When my father died," Nusrat said, "the group was looking for someone of that caliber to replace him. They could not find anyone. I had learned the music, but I wasn't actively practicing it. One day I dreamt that my father took me to a mosque in India, a place known as the 'Gathering.' He asked me to sing, and I said, 'I cannot sing.' And he said, 'Sing.' That's when I took my father's place as leader of the troupe."

It is said that the qawwal is the mouthpiece of divine power, a responsibility Nusrat accepted with reverence and humility. "We are trying," he said, "to portray a message of truth, humanity, love, and peace, to bridge the gap between Allah, the Almighty, and the human being. We try to uplift the human being and bring him closer to the Creator, Allah Almighty." He was surprised and pleased to see people in the West respond so strongly to his music, despite their inability to understand the Urdu lyrics. He saw himself on a sort of diplomatic mission, and as someone who spread the word of God. "Music," he said, voicing a truism that nevertheless has profound meaning for those working in little-known traditions around the world, "is an international language. It tells stories with rhythm and beat."

Nusrat recorded many different types of music, from traditional qawwali music with

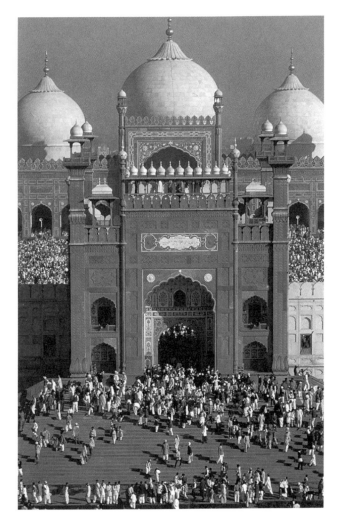

We are trying to portray a message of truth, humanity, love, and peace, to bridge the gap between Allah, the Almighty, and the human being. We try to uplift the human being and bring him closer to the Creator, Allah Almighty.

vocals, tablas, and harmoniums, to lovely, textured productions with Canadian guitarist Michael Brook, and even hip hop with British producer Bally Sagoo. Peter Gabriel used Nusrat's voice to great effect on his 1988 soundtrack for Martin Scorsese's film *The Last Temptation of Christ*. It was in part his willingness to try new things that won him so many enthusiasts outside of Pakistan. "It's a good thing," he said, referring to Massive Attack's "Mustt Mustt" remix. "This is another form of spreading the word and the music to the West." He later worked with Ry Cooder and Pearl Jam's Eddie Vedder on the haunting *Dead Man Walking* soundtrack, a performance that won him yet more admirers.

The aim of qawwali is transcendence. "Do not accept the heart that is the slave to reason," warn the lyrics to one qawwali song. "The heart," Nusrat said, "should not be a slave to anything." It is said that many people came to Sufism, to religion, through the beauty of Nusrat's music, and people sometimes went into trance states during his concerts. "If they listen with their hearts," he said, "Sufis and those who are not Sufis are bound to go into a trance, and they do. It has happened several times in Pakistan that people were carried away on stretchers and taken to the hospital. Doctors were called in to look at others. But it's also Sufi music that brings them back to normal reality. They went from the normal stage to the higher stage, and the music will calm them down again. To get people to that stage, to that intensity, I have to feel it first, and then I take the people with me. I am a kind of vessel that raises all of these people up for a short while."

In recent years, Nusrat had been battling health problems related to diabetes. He and his colleagues were already grooming a cousin, Rahat Fateh Ali Khan, to carry on the family tradition. En route to Los Angeles to receive a kidney transplant that might have saved his life, he died in London on August 16, 1997. He is deeply missed.

Amália Rodrigues

Amália Rodrigues is the undisputed Queen of Fado, the national song form of Portugal. Her legendary voice has an almost otherworldly intensity. "Amália," French writer André Maurois said in 1956, "is a phenomenon comparable only to Nijinsky." Whether storytelling in supple, delicate phrases about the common experiences of life or bursting into an elegant, full-throated wail against the cruelties of fate (the literal meaning of the Portuguese word *fado*), the force and passion in her voice is unmatched in the recorded history of the music.

Rodrigues has said that fado is about inexorable destiny, "the knowledge that one cannot fight one's fate, what can't be changed." Begun in Portugal by women singing about husbands or sweethearts who had left home as fishermen or as sailors on voyages of discovery, fado is based on musical traditions—Moorish, Jewish, Catholic—that go back centuries. Such music was also sung by the sailors to their faraway sweethearts. Like flamenco, it is an expression of profound feeling, especially of longing and loneliness—the blues. It is also linked to the Portuguese concept of *saudade*. Although it has no exact English translation, saudade represents complex feelings of yearning, homesickness, longing for past greatness, regret, and even guilt.

Amália Rebordão da Piedade Rodrigues was born in Lisbon in 1924, and grew up in the city's impoverished but culturally rich Alfama district. Her mother left when she was a year old, not to return until Rodrigues was fourteen. An early photograph shows the two standing together dockside selling fruit. "I used to sing everything," she once said. "I heard the blind beggars singing popular songs, and from my savings I always found some money to buy the sheet music for those songs."

Rodrigues's career began in 1939 at a fado club called Retiro da Severa, then one of the most fashionable night spots in Lisbon. She was soon working ten days a month for 500 escudos. By 1940, she had become a star, earning 1,000 escudos a night. In 1943, she went to Spain to perform and fell in love with flamenco. She traveled to Brazil in 1944, where she scored a huge hit at the Copacabana Casino, and cut her first 78-rpm records in Rio a year later. Her manager, José de Melo, refused to let her record in Portugal, thinking that if her fans could have her on vinyl, they wouldn't attend her shows. The first Portuguese recordings came in 1951 from the Melodia label. Her first international hit came with a live recording made at Paris's famed Olympia Theater in 1955. The song was "Coimbra," named for the graceful old Portuguese city; in English it was known as "April in Portugal."

With her greatest work behind her, Rodrigues retains the regal bearing of a great diva. Although she has ceased performing, she makes an occasional public appearance and worked behind the scenes to help promote the 1998 Lisbon World Expo. But she remains for the most part reclusive, in some ways resembling Marlene Dietrich in her later years, solitary, using only photos taken earlier in her career, looking back nostalgically as if fulfilling some implacable destiny.

Fela Anikulapo Kuti

I interviewed the late Fela Anikulapo Kuti in 1986, during his first trip to Los Angeles in seventeen years. A lot had happened since his first visit. He had become one of the best-known African musicians in the world, and one of the most controversial and outspoken. And in his native Nigeria—potentially one of the richest nations in Africa—he had been confronting one of the most corrupt governments in the world, naming collusive officials and organizations. Taunting them in his songs and speeches, he played a dangerous game of cat-and-mouse with Nigeria's notorious military leaders. He was beaten and imprisoned several times, and once narrowly escaped death at the hands of the Nigerian army.

Fela ("he who emanates greatness") Anikulapo ("one who carries death in a sack") Kuti ("he whose death cannot be caused by

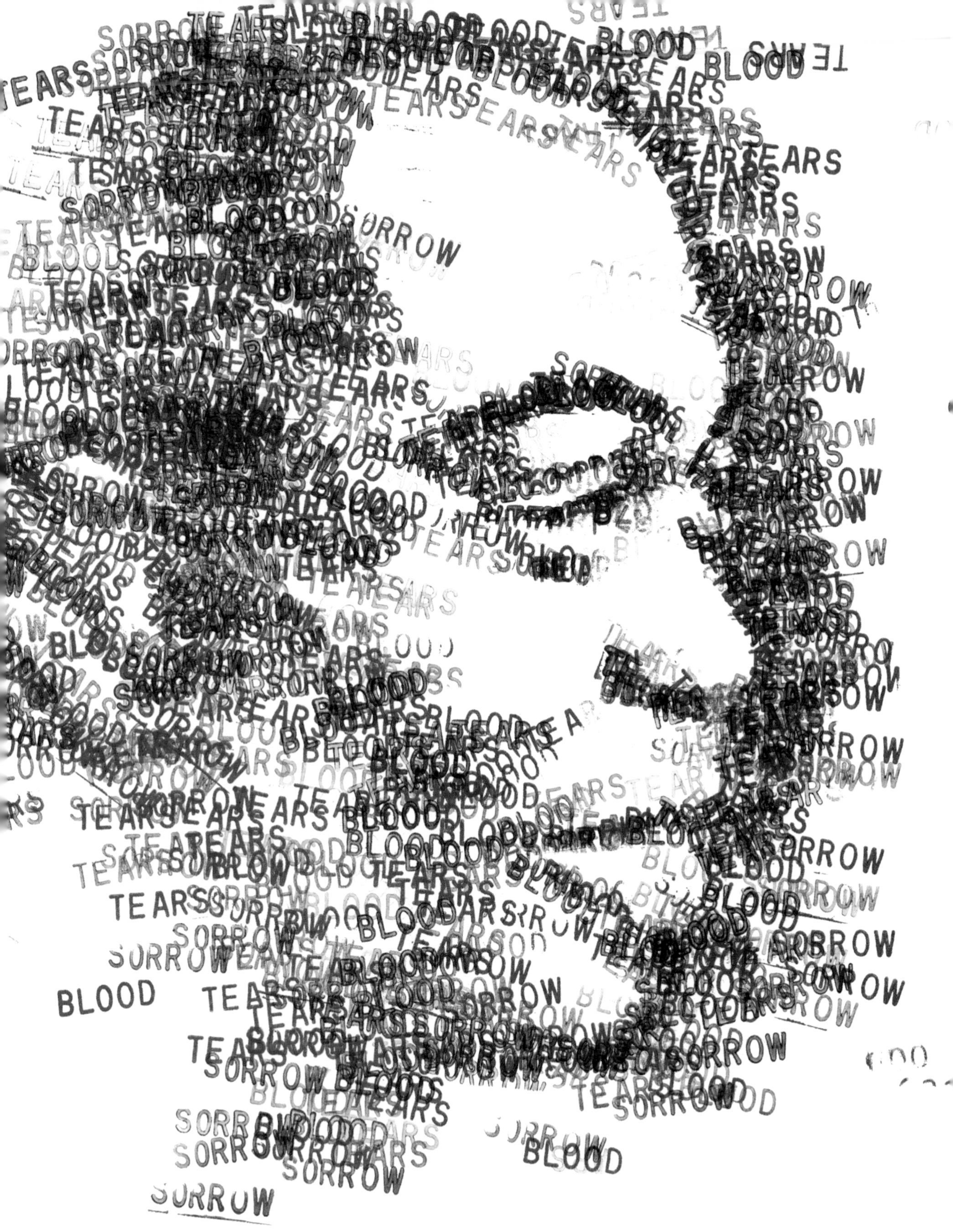

African leaders have put the lives of millions of Africans in danger because of their corruption in their own countries and because of the disunification of the continent.

the hand of man alone") was born in Abeokuta, Nigeria, in 1938 and raised in a respected middle-class Yoruba family. His father, the Reverend I. O. Ransome Kuti, was a composer and an Anglican minister. His mother, Funmilayo, was a central figure in the struggle for Nigerian self-rule and a fighter for women's rights. She traveled to China, where she is said to have met Mao, and was awarded a Lenin Peace Prize.

Fela told me about his sometimes troubled childhood, and described his difficult relationship with his parents, though not without humor. "My father was a very strict man," he said. "I thought he was wicked—he kicked my ass so many times. He had [strict] regulations at school. Can you imagine going to school for five years and not being allowed to lean on the walls? That was tough on my father. He was a great man. That was how he understood life should be. [Disciplined.] The little Bible, man—'Spare the rod, spoil the child,' you know. My mother, she was wicked too, man. I tell you, that woman. She had the strength of a man! And she whipped you like a man—'Touch your toes!' Systematic ass-kicking. Even though my father was wicked to me, I still liked him as a father. My mother I liked very much, too. You see, I couldn't connect the beatings that were given to me with their affection for me and the way I felt about myself, what was in my own mind. 'I'm not a bad boy. I don't have to keep asking [for permission] to do the right things.' But on the whole they were beautiful parents. They taught me everything, you know. They made me see

life in their own perspective, and if they had not brought me up with those experiences, I don't think I would have been what I am today. So the upbringing was not negative."

When Fela was twenty, he was sent to London to attend university, with the aim of becoming a medical doctor. Always the rebel, he had other ideas. When he arrived in England, he immediately dropped his pre-med studies to pursue music at the Trinity School of Music. In London, he listened to the music of Charlie Parker, Miles Davis, and John Coltrane, took up keyboards and trumpet, and began playing in jazz and funk bands. He returned to Nigeria in 1963 and formed his first band, Koola Lobitos.

When Fela visited Los Angeles in 1969, he played small clubs as a kind of cocktail lounge musician. He also became friends with a woman who changed his life, Sandra Izsadore. She introduced him to the Black Power movement and the Black Panthers, and helped him meet leaders like Stokely Carmichael, Angela Davis, and the Last Poets. A fully politicized Fela returned to Lagos the next year, where he recorded his first hit, "Jeun Ko'ku," Yoruban for "Eat and Die," and opened the Shrine Club. He soon became known for his confrontational music and political activity.

Talking about the impact of his sojourn in the U.S., Fela told the *New York Times* in 1977, "It was incredible how my head was turned. Everything fell into place, man. For the first time, I saw the essence of blackism. It's crazy; in the States people think the black power movement drew inspiration from Africa.

All these Americans come over here looking for awareness. They don't realize they're the ones who've got it over there. Why, we were even ashamed to go around in national dress until we saw pictures of blacks wearing dashikis on 125th Street."

At the time of our interview, Fela had just been freed, after eighteen months in prison in

the lower classes. It was a rough-edged, in-your-face sound. Seen live, his was a loose and swinging band, their ensemble arrangements never polished or too clean. Fela's bands would sometimes include twenty pieces, creating a huge wall of sound, and twenty of his wives would dance suggestively with him on stage. He would play his saxophone, both

Nigeria, and was happy to be back in the U.S. He talked about what it was like seeing Los Angeles for the first time since that momentous visit in 1969. "It does bring everything back," he said. "It's quite exhilarating to come back to the place where you had some heavy experiences in your life."

Like fellow West African Manu Dibango, Fela was an innovator. It was he who developed the style called Afrobeat, fusing the brassy horn sections of James Brown's famous bands with steady Yoruban rhythms and agit-prop lyrics that employed the pidgin English of

recite and sing his inflammatory rhetoric. For effect, someone might hand him a lighted cigarette, though he did not smoke. Fela did, however, enjoy smoking *igbo*—Nigerian marijuana—and often sang about it, much to the chagrin of the authorities.

Fela wrote many controversial songs. "Gentleman" lambasted Africans for wearing suits and ties while in Africa; "I.T.T.," or "International Thief Thief," alluded to the Nigerian government's involvement with the corporate giant IT&T; "Zombie" attacked the military mentality; "B.O.N.N."—"Beasts Of No

Nation"—spoke of world leaders as vicious animals covered with human skin. His criticisms were not ignored— he frequently became the target of the military government. On several occasions, the army attacked Fela's fortified compound in Lagos, which he called the Kalakuta Republic (*kalakuta* means rascal, a term prisoners use for each other). The worst of these attacks occurred in 1977, when his home was invaded by several hundred soldiers who brutally beat Fela and his wives and threw his 77-year-old mother from a second-floor window. (She died a few weeks later.) His musical equipment and master recordings were destroyed, and Fela himself suffered injuries that would have a lasting affect on his ability to play the saxophone and trumpet. Undaunted, Fela continued to write provocative songs that enraged the government while earning him ever larger domestic and international audiences.

Polygamy is still practiced in Nigeria, though it has also been a source of much controversy. On this subject too, Fela was typically outspoken. Following the events of 1977, he was sent into exile in Ghana. There he continued his political activity, and was subsequently forced back to Lagos. When he returned in 1978, Fela married twenty-seven women. In an interview in *Spin* magazine, he explained that he wasn't going to allow the institution of marriage to tie him down anymore. He wanted more freedom, and he wanted more women around him to break the jealous hold of the wives who had prevented him from being with other women. I asked him if he allowed his wives the same freedom. "What I'm really saying," he told me, "is that I do not believe anymore in the institution of marriage because for me, for the progress of the mind, it is evil. Why do people marry? Is it to be together? Is it to have children? What is the real reason people marry? Because they are jealous—people marry because they are possessive, because they are selfish. All this comes down to the very ugly fact that people want to own and control other people's bodies. They use marriage to do that. I think the mind of human beings should develop to a point where jealous feelings are completely eradicated."

In 1984, Fela was arrested at the Lagos airport on trumped-up charges of currency smuggling. "I was coming to America to play music. I was delayed at the airport, and they took me to the police station and locked me in a cell. The whole policy of the government then was that people like me should be incarcerated, so they jailed me for five years. [He spent eighteen months in prison.] I had been to court in Nigeria many times. I'm very popular in my country, so it seemed almost impossible to jail me. People could not believe it was possible, but the government wanted to prove they could do impossible things. They wanted to scare people, terrify the citizens, so I was sent to jail."

Fela believed that his imprisonment was meant to serve as an example, but he also felt that the Nigerian authorities wanted to prevent him from coming to the U.S. "They didn't want me to repeat the things I had said in Europe," he recalled. "Fela in America was not good for them at all, for their own outlook on things, which is quite a low, low outlook."

While in prison, Fela decided to run for political office, an ambition that he had often made public. In an interview for *News Watch* (a sort of Nigerian *Newsweek*) immediately following his release from prison, he said he felt that his experience in prison showed the Nigerian people the honesty of his struggle.

"When I was in prison," he told the magazine. "Many things happened that vindicated my views." In a tone reminiscent of the biting satire of his lyrics, he assured a London press conference that if elected he would employ a strategy of rudeness when faced with other African leaders: "Hey, Mobutu, how much did you steal today? . . . Cries of 'Thief! Mother-fucker!' will drown the speeches at summit meetings, and all Nigerians will immediately be enrolled in the army to eliminate violence." Although Fela declared himself a candidate and enjoyed a strong base of popular sup-port—other politicians often sought his endorsement—he did not officially run in the (highly suspect) 1988 Nigerian elections.

Fela often spoke of a unified Africa. "The way they behave in Africa now is negative to progress," he said. "The most oppressive aspect of this negativity is the division of Africa into small states such as Nigeria, Ghana, and so on. Ultimately, we need to unify Africa." I asked him about South Africa, which at that time was still suffering under the system of apartheid. "It is the division of Africa that encourages apart-heid," he said. "Once Africa is united, apart-heid will collapse immediately, but if Africa is divided, they can do what they like down there. African leaders have put the lives of millions of Africans in danger because of their corruption in their own countries and because of the dis-unification of the continent."

Fela died of heart failure in Lagos on August 2, 1997, due to complications from AIDS. The rampant corruption in Nigeria that he ridiculed so relentlessly remains the norm. Less than two years before Fela's death, the government of the late General Sani Abacha executed dissident writer Ken Saro-Wiwa and eight others. Only Fela's immense fame kept him from a similar fate. No less than ten pres-idents had ruled Nigeria since 1963, and Fela had antagonized several of them. Today, there is no one on the scene to continue Fela's work in the same flamboyant and urgent manner.

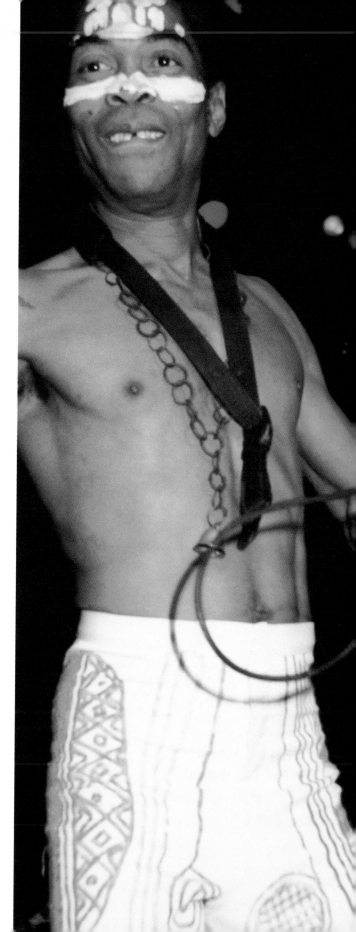

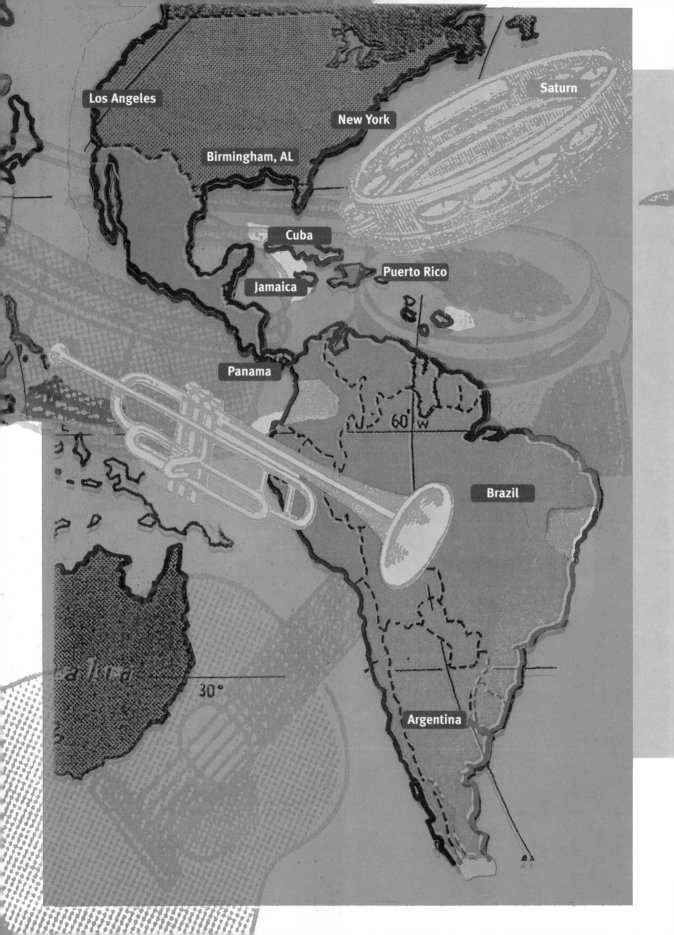

Rhythm Planet

Baaba Maal

Senegalese singer Baaba Maal is known for his dramatic vocal style and a unique way of blending traditional West African string and percussion instruments with slamming electric grooves. He carries on many of the Fulani musical traditions of northern Senegal, where he was raised, and has also incorporated into his music the folk and work songs of other regions. He is a riveting presence on stage, where he typically performs in beautiful traditional clothing, and his lyrics reflect a keen awareness of contemporary issues.

An artist of high principles, Maal has earned a reputation as an intellectual in Senegalese music. This is no small feat, since he was not born into the *griot* caste of the culture's storytellers and historians, which would traditionally have excluded him from becoming a musician. Fortunately, Maal's elementary school headmaster departed from tradition and encouraged all students to practice music. Maal's mother sang at local weddings and taught her son the traditional songs and dances of his people, and he was also encouraged musically by his father, a muezzin who

I believe that spirituality is more important than politics and material things. When you create a work, you must do it not for yourself but for every human being.

called people to worship at the village mosque. Listening to his father sing had a profound impact on Maal as a child, and his religious experiences shaped his attitude toward music. A good spiritual education, Maal insists, is necessary for an authentic life. "I believe that spirituality is more important than politics and material things," he says. "When you create a work, you must do it not for yourself but for every human being. I like material things, but material things must be built on spiritual belief. We have a proverb in our country: Any child who acquires material things easily, but doesn't have an education in spiritual matters, will never know how to use those material things."

Maal grew up in the village of Podor on the shore of the Senegal River, and from there went to the Senegal capital of Dakar to study art at the École des Beaux Arts. "African traditional music was everywhere in Africa," Maal says. "When I started singing, I wanted to learn more about this music, and to know more about other forms of music. At Beaux Arts I found that everything white people have in their music, in classical music and so on, we have in African music, but our way of doing it is not the same."

From Dakar, Maal went to France to study music at the Paris Conservatoire. "I was very curious to hear all kinds of music," he says. "I listened to the radio a lot because it was the time of the new Senegalese, Malian, and Mauretanian stations. [France opened its airwaves to independent stations in 1981.] I went to Paris to try to understand . . . to compare. I met fabulous musicians there. I discovered the reggae poet Mutabaruka, and played with musicians like Linton Kwesi Johnson. It was good experience to see how others managed and promoted their music."

Unlike Senegal's dominant *Wolof* music, which is based on a rhythmic groove, Maal's music emphasizes melody. Another famous Senegalese musician, Youssou N'Dour, sings in Wolof and makes music in the *mbalax* tradition, which is based in the port city of Dakar and infuses multiple styles into its mix. In

contrast, Maal's music is rooted in the ancient *yela* rhythm of northern Senegal, and is influenced by the wide empty spaces of the Sahel, the arid region between central Africa and the Sahara. Yela dates to the Fulani Empire of the eleventh century, when Islam was first introduced to the region, and there is an obvious Muslim influence in the music, especially in the way it is sung. "When something happened in the empire, they used to play [yela] to call people to listen," Maal explains. "If the king wanted to tell his people something important, they would play yela to bring people to listen." Yela is said to have evolved from the rhythm of the sounds made by women pounding grain, and was initially performed only by women. "They would beat on their calabashes to make the rhythm," Maal says, a rhythm he describes as similar to a reggae beat.

Along with Mansour Seck, Maal's nimble guitarist, Maal has modernized yela using Western instruments while preserving the melodies of traditional songs. "We've reintroduced into yela the *kora*, talking drum, *djembe*, and other African instruments," Maal says. The kora, a twenty-one string harp lute (a huge gourd wrapped in delicately beaded goatskin), is one of the most beautiful instruments in the world and a central instrument for much traditional West African music.

BABA MAAL

"Génération Nouvelle"

Any child who acquires material things easily, but doesn't have an education in spiritual matters, will never know how to use those material things.

Maal named his band Daande Lenol, or the Voice of the People. From the beginning, he has not been afraid to challenge traditional African values if he believes they are detrimental to modern African society. His first internationally distributed album, *Djam Leelii* (The Adventurers), was released on cassette in Senegal in 1984. The recording reached England in 1989, and attained legendary status among African music aficionados there. The album cover is significant. It shows a traditional African interior—an image that could be a hundred years old—with a boombox displayed prominently on a table. The title song speaks of the seasons and of common experiences in contemporary life in northern Senegal: "When a grain ripens to perfection, it must be harvested; otherwise the birds will eat it. So in life there is a right moment for everything. The saddest of times are the good-byes. When the land has dried up and there is not enough to keep young men at home, the Tukulor youth know they must leave for Gabon, or the Congo, or Ivory Coast or Burundi, or even Europe. Their future is uncertain; they don't know what they will find or when they will come back. But one thing is for sure: there is no reason for them to stay."

Although a student of all kinds of music, Maal has never strayed far from his roots. Like many international musicians, he is also wary of the categories often used to sell his music in the West. "I'm sometimes afraid to hear about 'World Music,' " he told interviewer Richard Trillo. "I'm afraid to see our music taken like a fish, hooked out of the water. I think it's important for people to have a name. But I don't want people to put African music or other kinds of music in a corner and say after all these other kinds of music you have this kind of music, and call it 'World Music.' No."

Madredeus

Fado—an ancient Portuguese urban folk style—is perhaps the least known "world music" today. But by fusing modern sounds with the soulful spirit of fado (literally "fate"), the six-member Portuguese band Madredeus has single-handedly revolutionized the style's status. With millions of albums sold and solid international notoriety, Madredeus has helped connect Portugal's past with its future, opening new explorations in

You allow yourself to feel the pain, because you feel
that this pain proves that you are alive and that
you still have feelings, and that's what allows you to be
open to future experiences.

sound while reviving interest in the country's traditional music.This is ironic since the band tried very hard to distance itself from fado at first, purposefully avoiding the Portuguese guitar used in Lisbon fado. When I talked at length about the history and different styles of fado with three of Madredeus's members, Pedro Ayres Magalhães, Francisco Rebeiro, and Gabriel Gomes, Rebeiro described his original distaste for the form. Typical of younger generations, he admits he couldn't focus on or truly appreciate the fado. That changed, however, when he met Teresa Salgueiro, the emotional voice of Madredeus. "She had been more influenced musically by it," he recalls. "She sang a lot of fado and taught me to appreciate it. Now, fado is very much a feeling for me."

Fado has evolved over hundreds of years, so it's easy to understand how it might be difficult to detach yourself from something that is so naturally part of your culture. "In our country," Magalhães muses, "almost everyone can sing at least one fado, or at least they think they can!" "Of course," Rebeiro concedes, "fado's something that's in our subconscious."

While Madredeus's music is not fado, the spirit of the form, particularly its quality of *saudade*, resonates strongly. Saudade is a word heard over and over in Portuguese, Lusafrican (the music of former Portuguese African colonies such as Cape Verde, Angola, and Mozambique), and Brazilian music. There is no exact translation; it is a mix of sadness, longing, and love. It's an emotion—one that is key in Portugal, with its long history of poverty and isolation. In Portugal, a once mighty seafaring nation that sent countless husbands and sons abroad to work and explore, it's no wonder fado tends to dwell nostalgically on the past, to speak sadly about the vast, mysterious oceans, to talk wistfully about things that once were but are no more.

These are all themes that figure in Madredeus's music: love, hope, travel, the sea, the distances that separate people, the freedom to be happy and the freedom to be sad, the horizon as an image of the future, life and death. This is, in Magalhães's words, "the wonderful world of saudade. Our legacy to the world; it is the Portuguese legacy." He describes saudade as a fantasy state, which connects us to past experiences we sometimes want to preserve even if they are painful. "You allow yourself to feel the pain," he says, "because you feel that this pain proves that you are alive and that you still have feelings and that's what allows you to be open to future experiences. All our music is made to fit that moment of fantasy while you are waiting." Of course, many of these themes have universal appeal, which is something the band intended.

Madredeus (pronounced ma-dray-DAY-oush) was cofounded in 1987 by Magalhães, a classical guitarist. Leader and chief lyricist, he added a second six-string guitar in favor of the Portuguese ten- or twelve-string instrument, an accordion, synthesizers, and a cello. The group didn't take off, however, until later that year, when they were joined by a young singer named Teresa Salgueiro. They had already auditioned fourteen singers when they discovering her singing an old fado in a Lisbon bar. They knew immediately that she was the missing element. Salgueiro was only seventeen at the time, with no formal vocal training, but she already had a voice of angelic purity. "A gift of nature," is how Magalhães described the discovery in a *New York Times* article. "Her voice really seemed to descend from the Portuguese masters," he tells me. Not only does Salgueiro possess a rich and otherworldly voice, but she emits an aura of absolute peace the audience often finds contagious. During her memorable performances, Salgueiro stands alone before the semicircle of other musicians, often austerely draped in black in the style of the great nineteenth-century Portuguese fado singer, Maria Severa.

When Madredeus first formed, they rehearsed in an old church in the Lisbon neighborhood of Madre de Deus, hence the group's name. Their first album, *Os Dias da Madredeus* (The Days of Madredeus), released in 1988, became an immediate European hit. *Existir* (To Exist), their second recording (and my favorite), came out in 1990. Their virtuosity and range of musical expression really comes through on the album's first three songs.

Lisboa (Lisbon), a two-CD live album, was released in 1993, followed by *O Espírito da Paz* (Spirit of Peace) the next year. English translations of the lyrics are included with the U.S. releases.

Their fifth CD, *Ainda* (the title means "still," as in "still going on" or "continuing"), was the soundtrack for Wim Wenders's film about Portugal, *Lisbon Story*. The film—"a sudden and welcome invitation," Magalhães muses—further expanded their reputation worldwide. A sixth recording, *O Paraíso* (Paradise), appeared in the U.S. in 1998.

Madredeus's success has been to combine lyrics that confront life's essentials with music that is delicate yet complex, like a fine filigree. They may have been able to escape the fado form, but not its spirit of saudade. All of the ancient form's soulfulness is present, but Madredeus's music is more contemporary and more complex. And with more than a million records sold around the world, Madredeus certainly has broader popular appeal. Indeed, the band has revitalized interest in traditional fado, just as Astor Piazzolla revived the tango.

Milton Nascimento

Milton Nascimento has made some of the most sublime music I've ever heard. I first encountered his art on Wayne Shorter's *Native Dancer* in 1975, but it was his Brazilian solo albums that really won me over. Hearing Nascimento's achingly pure falsetto was like watching a shooting star cross the sky. His plaintive ballads echo the feelings of millions of Brazilians.

Nascimento is from Três Pontas, a former gem mining capital that in 1750 boasted a larger population than New York City. Eventually, the gems disappeared, and Três Pontas went from a thriving colonial capital to a ghost town. In Minas Gerais, the towns are separated by mountains, and the music that comes from them is far from the happy, carefree sambas enjoyed by the inhabitants of Rio de Janeiro. In fact, someone hearing Nascimento's music for the first time might find it difficult to guess which country it came from. Blending his native Mineiro *toada*—a song characterized by a short stanza and refrain with a typically sentimental or melancholy melody and narrative lyrics—with strains of bossa nova, Gregorian chant, rock, *nueva canción*, samba, Portugal's *fado*, classical music, Andean music, and jazz,

> When I was little, I only liked the voices of women singing, because I felt that women sang with their hearts and the men wanted to show that they had good voices.

Nascimento, through his varied musical personality, has created a transcendental sound, capturing the attention of musicians and audiences worldwide.

Born in Rio de Janeiro, Nascimento moved to Três Pontas at the age of three with a family that had adopted him after his mother passed away. The only black child in a white family, Nascimento admits that he experienced racism from intolerant townspeople, but, he says, "I always knew how to keep things under control and transform them into something positive." The abundance of love and respect he received from his family no doubt had a lot to do with his positive outlook. "I owe everything I've done in my life to my parents. If I had to learn by myself what they have taught me, it would take two lifetimes."

Três Pontas featured prominently in Nascimento's growth as a musician. A small city in southern Minas Gerais, a mountainous inland state north of Rio, Três Pontas is, according to Nascimento, filled with musicians. And the area's geography has created great musical and cultural variation within the state. Minas Gerais also seems to have a peculiar effect on the psyche of its inhabitants. "They say that the music of the *mineiro*—a person from Minas Gerais—reflects the fact that there's no ocean in Minas," Nascimento told me, "and that the mineiro has to travel in his mind to see what's beyond the mountains." When I visited Minas Gerais, I felt a sort of loneliness there. The landscape is vast, the mountains immense.

When he was fifteen, Nascimento served a brief stint as a disc jockey, listening to and playing a wide range of music, from samba to mambo, rock, bolero, rumba, foxtrots, classical music, and jazz. In 1958, Nascimento heard João Gilberto for the first time, marking the start of a fascination with bossa nova and a lifelong respect for Gilberto.

"When I was little," he recalls, "I only liked the voices of women singing, because I felt that women sang with their hearts and the men wanted to show that they had good voices. I always liked the feminine voices, and I imitated several. The principle ones were a Brazilian singer named Angela Maria and Yma Sumac. As I grew up, my voice got coarser, deeper, and I didn't want it to change. But then Ray Charles came into my life, and João Gilberto, and I realized that men can sing too! Then I didn't have a problem."

Nascimento began performing in the late 1960s as part of a group of musicians in Belo Horizonte, the capital of Minas Gerais. They called themselves the Clube da Esquina—the Street Corner Club—and included guitarist Toninho Horta, keyboardist Wagner Tiso, lyricist Fernando Brant, and composer Lô Borges. The two albums they recorded, *Clube da Esquina 1* and *Clube da Esquina 2*, are now regarded as landmarks in Brazilian music. In his excellent book, *Masters of Contemporary Brazilian Song*, Charles Perrone describes what people have said about Nascimento's work: "Critics and reviewers of popular music and jazz around the globe have employed such adjectives as gripping, haunting, awesome, operatic, hypnotic, heartbreaking, and epochal to describe his art of singing. His music often

With Argentine singer Mercedes Sosa, Nascimento recorded Cuban *nueva canción* artist Silvio Rodríguez's "I Dream of Serpents" in 1980, during Brazil's military dictatorship. Faced with extreme censorship during that harsh time, many Brazilian musicians were forced into exile or left the country voluntarily. I asked Nascimento, who remained in Brazil, how the dictatorship affected him as a person and as an artist. "It was contrary to all of my beliefs about humanity," he recalls. "I was forced to defend my music to the bureaucrats. It got to a point on the album *The Miracle of Fishes* where, because my lyrics were censored, I was using my voice simply as an instrument, and still they wanted to know what I meant with the sound I was making! Sometimes they would censor a song, and we would change the name and send it back with the same lyrics, and they would let it go. They just wanted to shake us up."

It's difficult to imagine such discrimination against an artist who writes songs about hope, charity, brotherhood, and universal love—the most important values. I wondered if Nascimento was a religious man. "I don't belong to any religion," he explains, "but I believe in the soul of human beings, and that's what I try to convey in my music. I want to show people that we do have this soul and that we should try to show it more because often it stays hidden inside." Although most of his songs are sung in Portuguese, Nascimento believes that music is the "great universal language," and his goal is to reach others through his art. "All through my career," he says, "I've had many proofs that, yes, we can attain that goal of reaching people, even without thinking about the language. Songs in which we talk about friendship and love become like anthems in Brazil and in other countries too. And the beautiful thing about this, the thing I hope for most, is that when people hear my music, they find their own feelings within the songs. And that has happened; the music has really changed a lot of people."

seems to emit vibrations that come directly from the land through which it expands into a space that symbolically represents fields, mountains, valleys, which the voice tirelessly crosses without stopping."

Nascimento has achieved fame not only as a solo artist, but also through his many memorable collaborations. Jazz musicians in particular have been drawn to his melancholic tunes and challenging harmonies and vocal improvisations. By the late 1980s, Nascimento had recorded with Herbie Hancock, Paul Simon, Quincy Jones, Hubert Laws, Pat Metheny, Peter Gabriel, Ron Carter, and James Taylor, among others. One of my favorites is a piece called "Evocation of the Mountains," on the beautiful *Anima* album. (The album features Ricardo Silvera, Wagner Tiso, Robertino Silva, and Uakti, with guests Caetano Veloso and Simone.)

Bob Marley

Since his death in 1981 at age thirty-six, Bob Marley, who was at the time an international star, has become even more famous and revered. More of his recordings are sold today than during his lifetime. His image, forever charged with intensity and purpose, has become iconic.

Marley authored a musical movement that began in Jamaica and spread across the world, especially to developing countries. His message was taken to heart by millions of people, particularly the urban poor. When he died, his popularity was still on the rise, with his music embodying a powerful blend of very popular and danceable songs that spoke of love and vehemently railed against injustice.

Robert Nesta Marley was born in 1945 in the rural Jamaican town of St. Ann's Parish, the child of Cedella Booker, a Jamaica native, and Captain Norval Marley, a white colonial. Captain Marley married Booker when he learned of her pregnancy but soon abandoned her. Marley was a teenager when he and his mother moved to the Kingston housing development known as Trenchtown, a ghetto built on top of what was once the city dump. It was here that Marley was exposed to jazz and bebop and became associated with Joe Higgs, Jamaica's first indigenous recording artist and a reggae pioneer who deserves to be far better known. Higgs took the talented boy under his arm, teaching him about music and Rastafarianism. Marley began to take part in Higgs's backyard music sessions, and by 1962 was already making records. He soon formed a group with Bunny Wailer and Peter Tosh called the Wailers, so called because, as victims of the ghetto, they were born wailing.

Producer Chris Blackwell played a key role in the Wailers' success. Equally important was the production wizardry of Lee "Scratch" Perry. The release in 1973 of both *Burnin'* and *Catch a Fire* brought Marley and the Wailers a large following. Wailer and Tosh then went solo and Marley formed a new Wailers band. With them, he went on to record *Natty Dread* (1974), *Rastaman Vibration* (1976), and *Exodus* (1977), and Marley became an international star.

Preceded by ska, reggae music became hugely popular in England in the 1960s, hitting big in America in the 1970s. It was the first popular music not to come from an anglophile rock or folk group and opened people's minds to the world music explosion that followed in the 1980s with bands like that of King Sunny Ade.

Marley was a poet and musician's musician. He wrote songs of incendiary power, simplicity, and uncompromising honesty that inspired many bands that followed and helped to politicize musicians from South Africa to Brazil and Australia. An extremely charismatic performer, Marley galvanized listeners all over the world, and his commentary on the social and political upheavals of our time continues to be relevant. "You entertain people who are satisfied," he once said. "Hungry people can't be entertained—or people who are afraid. You can't entertain a man who has no food."

Youssou N'Dour

Not only was Youssou N'Dour born with a beautiful voice, he also inherited a singing tradition that gives him and his music a rich sense of Senegalese history. His mother, Ndeye Sokhana Mboup, was a *griotte*, or singing historian, famous in the Medina district of Dakar for her exquisite voice. His father, Elimane N'Dour, was a mechanic. "There was always music at home, day and night," he told me when I first met him in 1989. "I grew up in a neighborhood that was very poor, but very warm—everybody knew each other. This neighborhood was very close to the modern area where all the rich people were; my music opposes and transcends all the things that the rich people had." Growing up, N'Dour listened to a lot of soul music—James Brown and Marvin Gaye. "I was also blown away by Latin music," he says, "because there were always African elements mixed in."

As a boy, N'Dour was something of a local phenomenon. He sang at traditional gatherings and won a talent show in Dakar at age fourteen; the next year he was performing before large audiences. At sixteen he joined a local band, Diamono, and by seventeen he was asked to join the Star Band at Dakar's Miami nightclub. With his strong voice and

I think music is a more powerful force than politics.
In my music, and in African music, the message is
conveyed by the rhythm; that's what people feel.

good looks, he soon became immensely popular, earning large sums of money just out of
his teens. In 1979, he and several other musicians started their own band, Étoile de Dakar
(Star of Dakar), renamed a few years later
Super Étoile de Dakar. It remains Senegal's
leading group.

N'Dour has become the international star of
mbalax, a percussion-driven, seven-beat rhythmic style based on the interplay of Senegal's
indigenous *sabar* and *bugarbu* drums. The
style, a *Wolof* (the principal ethnic group and
official language of Senegal) music, was developed in the late 1970s by the Star Band. At
the time, Dakar was the center of many
trends, including the infatuation with Cuban
music, both on records and performed in
nightclubs by bands like Orchestra Baobab
and Super Diamono. While he was certainly
influenced by this sound, N'Dour wanted to
produce a distinctly African music, especially
in light of Senegal's independence, achieved
in 1960, the year following N'Dour's birth. He
added jazz inflections to Cuban horns and
used traditional singing techniques such as
scat, *bakou*-trilling (a traditional chant), and
tasso (a kind of rap) to create a full and very
rhythmic sound—dance music at its best.

N'Dour became an urban *griot*. Traditionally,
griots sang at ceremonies in praise of their
chiefs. They were rewarded with gifts and
money. Contemporary griots have redirected
their praise from chiefs and warriors to contemporary heroes, such as political leaders and
soccer stars, and even car manufacturers. The
heroes fulfill their traditional role by lavishing

the griots with money and gifts, which account
for a large portion of a griot's livelihood.

By 1983, N'Dour had his own nightclub in
Dakar, Thiosanne, where he performed six
nights a week. A turning point in his career
came in 1984 during a trip to London when
Peter Gabriel heard him play in a small club.
N'Dour's voice "sent shivers down my spine,"
Gabriel later told the *Wall Street Journal*. He
invited N'dour to sing on his 1986 album *So*
and had Super Étoile join him on his world
tour. That same year N'Dour played drums on
Paul Simon's *Graceland*.

N'Dour's first solo international recording,
The Lion, produced by George Acogny, was
released by Virgin in 1987. It includes a curious song called "Old Tucson." I asked N'Dour
what it was about. "When I visited Tucson," he
said, "and I saw the deserts and the remnants
of the Old West, I couldn't believe it. I visited
a lot of museums, and saw a lot of history
about American slaves. When I was little, I
loved Westerns, so I decided to write a song
about the past, about history. It made me
think of the history of slavery, of the island of
Gorée off the coast of Senegal where the
slaves were sent off."

On *The Lion*, N'Dour also sang a beautiful
duet in Wolof and English with Peter Gabriel,
"Shakin' the Tree," about women's rights in
Africa. In other songs, he has dealt with issues
such as the dumping of toxic waste in Africa,
political corruption, poverty, hunger, and disease—issues more often addressed by reggae
bands than by mainstream African groups. It
wasn't surprising when N'Dour was chosen to

be Africa's representative on Amnesty International's 1988 Human Rights Now Tour. "I think music is a more powerful force than politics," N'Dour said of the tour. "If it touched a few people, then it served its purpose. In my music, and in African music, the message is conveyed by the rhythm; that's what people feel."

While much of N'Dour's music comes from Wolof mbalax roots music, his collaborations have brought him wide recognition. He has sung in French and English, and toured with stars like Japan's Ryuichi Sakamoto. His latest album, *The Guide (Wommat)*, featured Branford Marsalis and Neneh Cherry, as well as a cover of Dylan's "Chimes of Freedom." The recording went gold in France, where N'Dour is a major star (he composed the theme song for the 1998 World Cup soccer tournament there), and sold more than 700,000 copies worldwide. Though he has yet to break through in the U.S., N'Dour continues to reach new fans beyond his core audiences in Senegal and Paris. However, unlike many other successful

African musicians who have settled abroad, N'Dour has steadfastly chosen to remain in Senegal and has built a state-of-the-art recording studio in his Dakar home. "It's very important to work in your country," he told the *New York Times*. "The work, the friends, that reality is reflected in our music."

Astor Piazzolla

Composer, bandleader, and unparalleled master of the accordionlike bandoneón, Astor Piazzolla devoted his life to the tango, the musical soul of Argentina. What the legendary Carlos Gardel had made internationally popular in the 1930s, Piazzolla transformed into a contemporary art form. Throughout a career that spanned nearly six decades, he extended the boundaries of the tango, often against fierce opposition. He was one of Latin America's most gifted composers, but, to those who were privileged to hear him play, he is also remembered as a musician whose sublime performances often reduced entire audiences to tears.

I first heard Piazzolla perform at the Montreal International Jazz Festival in 1986. I was new to his music. Like many others, I had been grabbed by his first internationally successful album, *Tango: Zero Hour*, when it appeared earlier that year on the small American Clavé label. I was moved by a beautiful slow piece on the recording, "Milonga del Angel," but I was devastated by Piazzolla's live performance. He played music of stupefying emotional intensity and heartbreaking romance. Dressed in black, with the serpentine bandoneón stretched over his knee,

I ran home and started writing tangos like crazy from that moment on. That day I started believing in Astor Piazzolla.

he was a commanding presence on that Montreal stage.

Piazzolla was born in 1921 in the seaside resort of Mar del Plata, 250 miles south of Buenos Aires. In 1923, his father took him and his mother to New York City, where they lived for the next fourteen years. It was there that the young Piazzolla received his musical training. His first bandoneón was a birthday gift from his father, who bought the instrument in a pawn shop for eighteen dollars.

Piazzolla's unique playing style and original sound evolved primarily from his early study of classical music. "I used to sit in my backyard in New York," he recalled, "and listen to a Hungarian pianist who was a concert player. His name was Bela Wilda. He studied with Sergei Rachmaninoff, and used to play three or four hours of Bach every morning. I used to get up and open the window and listen to this man play the piano. And I told my mother I wanted to study music with this man, not the other man who wanted to teach me to play tangos. So I went to study with Bela Wilda, and he adapted all his piano music to my instrument, the bandoneón. The piano has eighty-eight notes, and the bandoneón has seventy-eight. It's nearly like a piano. So I started playing Bach, Schumann, Mozart. My beginning was all classical music."

Piazzolla was also exposed to contemporary jazz, and he remembers learning to play Gershwin, but it was his father's love of the tango that would eventually shape his career. "I feel the tango," he said, "because my father had fifty or sixty 78-rpm records, and they were all tangos. Very good orchestras. My father used to listen to them every night, and he would cry. I looked at him and I couldn't imagine why he cried. Then he said, 'This is the music that I feel, that I love most. This is the music from Argentina. This is the tango.' And little by little, fourteen years listening to that music every evening when my father came back from work, I started to feel it myself. So that's why I went

> People would come into the clubs and insult me.
> They would threaten me with guns. In Argentina you
> can change anything but the tango.

back to Argentina and was struck by this music called the tango. But the ones who wanted to strike me were the traditional tango players, who didn't like my way of playing."

The bandoneón is the instrument par excellence of tango. Though small at first glance, it is nearly five feet wide when fully extended. In place of a keyboard are buttons on both sides. "The story of the bandoneón is very strange," Piazzolla explained. "It was invented in 1854 in Krefeld, Germany, to play religious music in a very small church, because they didn't have any money to buy an organ. So the bandoneón has a very sad, melancholic sound. The left hand especially sounds like an organ." By 1890, he continued, the instrument had found its way into the brothels of Buenos Aires, where it was used to play tangos. From there the instrument went into the concert halls. "Then," Piazzolla recalled with a laugh, "I went back and played it in the church in Krefeld."

"A complicated instrument," in Piazzolla's words, the bandoneón has four different sounds. The buttons on the left hand have one tone when the instrument is opened, and another when it closes. The same is true for the right hand. In Piazzolla's hands, the bandoneón developed a haunting quality; his music is deep, moody, and mysterious.

An auspicious event in Piazzolla's early career was a 1934 meeting with the world's most famous tango singer Carlos Gardel. "We were ten Argentines living in New York then," Piazzolla recalled. "When Carlos got there, it was like God coming to New York. He was the best tango singer. And my father, who used to

make sculptures of wood, made a sculpture of an Argentine gaucho playing the guitar, and he dedicated it to Carlos Gardel. I went to his hotel and gave him this sculpture from my father. When he found out I was playing the bandoneón, he nearly fainted, because he couldn't find a bandoneón player any place, especially not in New York. I wasn't the best bandoneón player, I was the *only* bandoneón player! So I was playing all classical music, and he said, 'Can you play a tango?' I said, 'If I can play Johann Sebastian Bach, I can play a tango. It's much easier.'" Though Piazzolla was only thirteen, Gardel hired him to play in *El día que me quieras*, one of his last films. It was the first time he had ever played a tango.

At sixteen, Piazzolla returned with his family to Argentina, settling in Buenos Aires, and he continued his studies. By night he played and arranged for Anibal Troilo, leader at the time of one of the country's most popular tango orchestras. He also studied for seven years with composer Alberto Ginastera.

In 1954, a symphony Piazzolla wrote for the Buenos Aires Philharmonic won him a government scholarship to study in Paris under the celebrated composition teacher Nadia Boulanger. "She was my second mother," Piazzolla said. "She didn't only teach me music, she taught me life. She taught me to believe in myself. She told me to throw the classical music that I wrote into the garbage. 'Throw it away. This is no good. I can't find Piazzolla in this classical concert music.' She wanted to know what I really did in life, what I did for a living. I was very much ashamed to tell her that I played tango, and above all I wouldn't dare say, 'I play the bandoneón.' I thought she would throw me out the window. I was there studying like [other Boulanger students] Aaron Copland, like Leonard Bernstein and Igor Markevich. How can I say to this old and wonderful lady that I was playing tango in a café in Buenos Aires? All of a sudden I had this moment of courage and I said, 'Look, Miss Boulanger'—she was 75 years old then—'Look,' I said, with my head bending down, 'I play tango.' 'Oh,' she says, 'that's beautiful.'

"I was amazed at her answer, but she loved tango. She started naming all the tangos she knew—Stravinsky's, and Darius Milhaud's—so many important composers in the world wrote tangos. She said, 'You don't play piano?' 'No,' I said, 'I just use piano for composing.' 'What do you play?' I was again ashamed, and I said, 'I play the bandoneón.' She said, 'Oh, I love the bandoneón. Did you hear Kurt Weill when he played the bandoneón?' 'Yes,' I said. 'Boris Blacher also used the bandoneón, and Hindemith wrote for the bandoneón.' She wanted to know about my tangos. I played a little bit of my tangos, and she took my two hands together and said, 'This is Astor Piazzolla. Don't ever leave it.' I ran out of her apartment, racing down four flights of stairs, more happy than I had ever been. I ran home and started writing tangos like crazy from that moment on. That day I started believing in Astor Piazzolla, and I threw away all the music I had written. I thought I was a genius because I wrote symphonies, but I wasn't a genius because I wasn't Astor Piazzolla."

Piazzolla returned to Buenos Aires in 1955 and formed his own band. His new music, which he called *nuevo tango*, departed sharply from traditional tango. It was passionate, bitter, tender, wildly emotional music influenced by twentieth-century classical innovations (he loved Stravinsky) and jazz (he recorded with Gerry Mulligan and vibraphonist Gary Burton, among others). This new work drew intense

criticism. Even his own parents berated him. "When I started playing in Buenos Aires in 1955," he once said, "it was war—everyone was against me. The classical people wouldn't admit me to their world because they thought I was a dance-band player, and the popular musicians said I was classical. People would come into the clubs and insult me. They would threaten me with guns. In Argentina you can change anything but the tango." Many years later he would say, "It was a war of one against all, but in ten years, the war was won."

Piazzolla left Argentina to live in Paris in 1974, returning occasionally to perform, and moved back at the end of the dictatorship there in 1985. He wrote more than 750 compositions, including concert and chamber pieces, operas, film scores, and a cello sonata for Mstislav Rostropovich. (It was Piazzolla who brought the tango into the cello repertoire.) Although he made over 70 albums, many of his compositions were first recorded only after his death in 1992. At least fifty recordings of his work have been made since, including recent albums by world-class virtuosi like cellist Yo Yo Ma—who recorded a collection of Piazzolla classics, *The Soul of the Tango*, with members of Piazzolla's celebrated sextet—and violinist Gidon Kremer.

"When we speak of beauty, the beauty of architecture, of art, of people, of love," Kremer has said, "we must also invoke Astor Piazzolla's music. I believe in it because it evokes a better world through the language of nostalgia—in one single tango."

Tito Puente

Tito Puente, now in his mid-seventies, has probably done more to further the cause of Latin music than any other musician. Along with Machito, Puente took music from Puerto Rico and Cuba, added a sophisticated and cosmopolitan spin, and brought it to the world. He skillfully arranged and recorded many swing classics and popular songs in a Latin style, bringing the music to new fans who weren't necessarily dancers or frequenters of Latin clubs. He has been influential both as a composer, with an unprecedented run of hits in the 1950s that helped define the golden era of Latin music, and as a virtuoso *timbalero* whose speed and agility set a new standard for the instrument. With four Grammy awards, more than one hundred recordings as a bandleader, and a career that spans six decades, Puente is not only the Mambo King, he's the King of Latin Jazz. He is still a percussionist of commanding virtuosity, and his skills as an

arranger of jazz standards with a Latin groove are legendary. At an age when most people are long retired, he tours the world each year and shows no sign of slowing down.

I was very rhythmically inclined at a young age, always banging on cans and walls. The neighbors came in and told my mother, "Put that kid in school. Get him out of the house. Have him learn the drums."

I'm surrounded by a lot of talented and creative people who encourage me to be creative. That's how you get to make a hundred and seven albums.

Puente's parents were born in Puerto Rico. He was born Ernesto Antonio Puente Jr. in New York City's Spanish Harlem, a place that nurtured several Latin music masters, including Eddie Palmieri, Arsenio Rodríguez, and Noro Morales. A precocious child, Puente was enrolled in piano and dance lessons at an early age. "I was very rhythmically inclined at a young age," Puente says, "always banging on cans and walls. The neighbors came in and told my mother, 'Put that kid in school. Get him out of the house. Have him learn the drums.' So she did. Thanks to her, I went to study drumming. I started on piano, really. Then I switched over to drums, percussion. And eventually, I got into timbales, and that's where I developed my style."

In the late 1920s and 1930s, New York's *El Barrio*—Spanish Harlem—was home to many African-Americans as well as Latinos, and became a hothouse of musical creativity and cultural exchange. Puente was introduced to jazz and Latin music, and he remains indebted to those influences. I asked Puente to tell me more about his childhood influences: Did the Puente household keep a radio on? Did he hear anyone who made him want to become a musician? He answered immediately: "The big bands, naturally. The Stan Kenton Orchestra, Woody Herman, Duke Ellington, the Basie Band, any Cuban music, lots of Orquesta Casino de la Playa, Arsenio Rodríguez, some of the great Cuban bands too. I was into everybody at that time."

Puente gave his first professional performance in 1935, when he was just sixteen years old. "My first gig was with Noro Morales," he recalls. "I was sent in as a substitute for a drummer who got sick and recommended me to him at the Stork Club, a very big club on the east side of New York. In those days, the Latin band, the rumba band, was a relief band. When the society band or the fox-trot band got off, the relief rumba band used to take over and play. But we had to play everything: tangos, waltzes, fox trots, polkas. That's where you gain your experience, actually—playing, not reading books. You got to get on the street and play."

During the day, Puente went to school; at night his father took him to the club. "By eleven o'clock, I was already sleepy," he says. "I used to fall asleep on the drums, and sometimes the musicians would tie my foot to the pedal. They were always playing jokes on me." I asked him if he was scared, playing with Noro Morales and Machito at such a young age. "Yes and no. I never took my eyes off the leader. 'Cause if I'd miss a cue to go into the mambo or the coda, they'd go, 'Hey, that kid—get him out of here! He's not experienced.' But, then, you know, I was way ahead of them at the time anyway, 'cause I was watching them. I gained a lot of experience with Noro and with Machito, Pupi Campo, and José Curbello—a lot of bands, really, over the years."

Puente's first dream was to be a dancer, and were it not for an injury, the world might have missed out on his great musical gifts. "I loved dancing," he says. "I wanted to dance like Fred Astaire and Ginger Rogers, and used to do the carioca and the continental and tango and all that. But then my ankle got sprained, so I decided to get into the music. I'd loved music all my life, so I'm happy that happened. I play for dancers now. That's where I get my big kicks, watching dancers dancing to the music." Puente has seen many great dancers over the years. "There where so many of them," he says. "I believe in dancing. I feel that dancing makes the music, actually, because whatever you play, if you don't have any dancing, the music doesn't become popular. That's what happened, for instance, with the bossa nova, which was very popular musically but the steps mixed everybody up. They didn't know the steps, so we lost the music."

During World War II, Puente worked as a bandleader on a Navy ship. He recalls those days cheerfully: "Anytime new men came aboard, we'd ask 'em, do you play an instrument? If they said 'yeah,' we'd put 'em in the band right away. I was more or less in charge of that department. I already knew when I was on the ship that I was an arranger. I was performing in the band, playing saxophone and drums, and arranging." In 1945, Puente sailed into Tokyo Bay on the USS *Santee* when General MacArthur and Emperor Hirohito signed the treaty ending the war.

After three years at sea, Puente went back to New York City and enrolled at Juilliard. He didn't stay long. By then he was already deeply involved with Latin and popular music and Juilliard was, as he describes it, "ultraclassical . . . and my heart and soul wasn't into that. Then I got my own private teacher. I learned from Richard Bender, and developed my style that way." Miles Davis was at Juilliard at around the same time and had a similar experience; he needed to go out and play in

all the musicians do is play music," he says. "That's all they do thirty-four hours a day—practice. They learn all those things by ear. They don't even need sheet music any more, so it's a difficult thing for us to play. Here we have to do a lot of rehearsing to play like they do."

Puente often played at the Palladium, one of New York's hottest clubs in the 1950s and 1960s. "That was the home of the mambo," he recalls. "Everybody who loved Latin music used to come to the Palladium four days a week, Wednesday through Saturday. It was only a block up from Birdland, jazz corner of the world. People who came into New York for a Broadway show, let's say a matinee on Wednesday, would have dinner then come to the Palladium and catch a show with dancers. It was very exciting and very competitive—dancing and music—because for many years we had the great Machito band there, and Tito Rodriguez, naturally, and myself."

Today on Fifty-Third Street, parking garages fill the space formerly occupied by the Palladium and Birdland. Although he definitely lives and works in the present, Puente gets nostalgic when he sees the newer buildings. "As time passes, I get a lot of young people asking me how it was during that era," he says. "And I always tell 'em it will never come back. Naturally it was a beautiful era for music and dancing, the development of musical sounds. Same thing for jazz."

With six decades onstage, I wondered where Puente found the inspiration to keep up his hectic life, much of which is still spent in hotel rooms. "I do a lot of traveling," he says,

the clubs. They didn't meet at Juilliard, but later had many opportunities to meet and perform together. Puente remembers Davis fondly: "Miles Davis and I were friends for many years. In fact, at the last concert we did together, at the Newport Jazz Festival, the third tune I performed was 'All Blues.' We were in the dressing room and he told me—I'll never forget it—he always told me [impersonating Davis's rasp], 'Tito ah love the way you play "All Blues,"' man, rare and crazy. You give it that sexy treatment.' I'll never forget him. For my third tune in every show, I look up, think about him, and dedicate 'All Blues' to Miles."

Puente has performed and recorded with many of the great Cuban musicians and singers, including Celia Cruz, Santos Colon, Tito Rodriguez (once an arch rival), Alfredo de la Fé, La India, Vicentico Valdes, and the Fania All Stars. Though he never performed in Cuba before the 1959 revolution, he has traveled there several times since then to play with contemporary Cuban musicians. Like many musicians, Puente is awed by the Cubans, commenting that when American musicians hear Cuban musicians play, they feel they have to go back to school. "In Cuba "a couple of million miles a year, you know, but I'm surrounded by a lot of talented and creative people who encourage me to be creative. That's how you get to make a hundred and seven albums. Each album has got to be interesting. What's next? I don't know. Maybe the next thing I need is to be the first to play the moon in the year 2000."

Puente is tireless in his devotion to his art. He finds himself a role model to a lot of young people, and established a scholarship fund nearly twenty years ago. He feels happy to have helped many young players throughout his career. He has five honorary university degrees, and he says he'd like to remain a role model "until the point that [Latin] music gets the recognition it deserves around the world."

I asked him if he thought the crowds coming to hear Latin music had changed. "Whenever I do a concert in, say, Cheyenne, Wyoming, there's always a big place with sawdust on the floor. And because the *Mambo Kings* movie went there, some cowboy will come up to me and say, 'I seen you, Mr. Puente. Could you play me a saltza?' So I turn around and say, 'This guy wants a saltza.' The music is getting around, and people love it; they love the percussive end of it.

We have no language problems anymore. 'I don't care what language you sing in, as long as you play the rhythm.' That's how people feel. And especially in jazz; people relate to so many jazz melodies. And you give 'em the Latin treatment, you combine 'em both—that's the marriage that Dizzy did with Cuban music and bebop—and that's what makes the music so popular."

One thing that Puente has done best is arrange. His talent and versatility as an arranger has enabled him to work with a vast range of musicians outside the Latin arena, including George Shearing, the Count Basie Orchestra, and Woody Herman. I've always admired Puente's ability to take just about any song and turn it into great Latin music. "Sure I can," he says. "And when these young people go home, they say, 'Mom! You know that guy you were talking about, the one you used to hear at the Palladium? He was great, he was wonderful.' I gotta lay it down and play well for them too. At the universities that I play, at the jazz festivals, they only give us a certain amount of time, a little taste, a little tinge—those forty-five minutes that I have, I really pick them up, you know, and that's important."

Celia Cruz

I remember Celia Cruz striding onto the huge stage of the Hollywood Bowl in 1996 in a lobster fantail evening gown with a headdress that would have put Erykah Badu out of business. She sang, danced, and toyed with the adoring audience for over ninety minutes. Her voice resonated with great range, dynamics, rhythm, perfect diction, and beautiful intonation. Critics of many persuasions agree that Celia Cruz is the greatest female Cuban singer. Like Mambo King Tito Puente, she has recorded prodigiously, with more than one hundred albums and counting. And, like Puente, she travels constantly, performing in the world's great concert halls and clubs.

No reference works cite Celia Cruz's age and she won't give it, but by now she has been performing professionally for more than fifty years. The Queen of Salsa was born in Havana. Her singing started with lullabies to her siblings. When she sang at home, neighbors often came to listen and were amazed. She studied literature at a teacher's college, and went on, around 1945, to pursue classical studies at Havana's National Conservatory of Music. She once remarked that she enjoyed the courses in harmony, theory, solfège, and piano technique, but she didn't like having to cut her nails. Her mother and her conservatory teachers encouraged her musical pursuits. Her father, on the other hand, did not want her to become a singer, thinking it a dishonorable profession. Cruz's mother prevailed, and supported her daughter's fledgling career.

In 1947, Cruz was prodded by a cousin into participating in a talent show, La Hora del Té, on Radio García Serrá. She won and became friends with Roderico Neyra, choreographer at Havana's famous Tropicana Nightclub, where she began performing with the show during the winter seasons. Cruz's recording career took off in the early 1950s with records for the Panart label, and she later began a lengthy association with the great *son* band, La Sonora Mantancera. After the 1959 revolution, she and the band left for America, where she has remained.

Cruz seems the incarnation of everything Cuban. Her way of speaking Spanish, as seen in the film about Cuban music, *Yo Soy Del Son a la Salsa*, seems quintessentially Cuban: fast, rhythmic, strong, and filled with enthusiasm and humor—a seamless extension of the way she sings. She is extremely versatile, and during her long and illustrious career she's performed many kinds of music, from classic son to commercial salsa and the sacred *santería* music derived from Yoruba tradition. Presumably well into her seventies, Cruz is a performer of radiant energy and has earned, many times over, her place in the pantheon of great divas.

Oumou Sangare

With her unique style and a powerful message, Oumou Sangare stands out among a field of successful female Wassoulou singers. "Her voice is an otherworldly thrill," says the *The New Yorker*. "When she lets fly one of her serpentine, earth-shattering phrases, you can almost hear the continents quake." Tall, striking, outspoken, an inspiration to her generation and to her sex—her lyrics lambast polygamy and call for freedom of choice in marriage for women—Sangare is a voice to be reckoned with.

Oumou Sangare sings for the women of Mali and, as she says, for those of all of Africa. "African women do not have as many rights as men," she said upon the release of her third album, *Worotan*. "It is the African woman who is responsible for the house, the children, everything. But if that woman wants to speak in the society, she is not listened to. So I sing her cause." From the beginning of her career, Sangare has voiced women's concerns. Her first album, *Moussolou* (Women), released in 1990, sold more than 200,000 copies, and by the age of twenty-one Sangare was a star in West Africa and well on her way to international fame. "I want to encourage them," Sangare says about the

women to whom her work has been dedicated, "to make them feel proud to be women. We have to fight and be dynamic."

Sangare was born in Bamako, the capital of Mali, in 1968. Her mother was also a singer, and she recognized Sangare's talent at an early age. "Sing like you're at home in the kitchen," her mother told her before her first performance, at Bamako's huge Stade des Omnisports, at the age of six. Like many future Malian stars, she began her career with the National Ensemble of Mali. She then joined the traditional Malian percussion group Djoliba and toured Europe in 1986. After the tour, Sangare returned to Mali resolved to form her own band and base her music on the southern Malian Wassoulou traditions of her homeland.

While encouraging the women of her country to employ freedom of choice in marriage, Sangare is also outspoken in her stance against polygamy. Her mother was one of three wives, and the experience of growing up in such a household affected her deeply. "I come from a polygamous family," she says. "In Mali, men are allowed to have up to four wives. But in this type of relationship, nothing works. The kids don't get along, there is a lot of jealousy between the wives and mothers, and the husbands aren't comfortable either. Everybody winds up suffering. This is why I can't stand it."

Sangare's recordings leave no doubt about where she stands on these and other issues. She is also justly famous for her songs about love and passion. In 1993, she released her second album, *Ko Sira* (Marriage Today), and *Worotan* (Ten Kola Nuts, a reference to the traditional price of a bride in Mali) appeared in 1996. Sangare's success has been instrumental in introducing the unique Wassoulou style of music to the rest of the world.

I come from a polygamous family. In Mali, men are allowed to have up to four wives. But in this type of relationship, nothing works. The kids don't get along, there is a lot of jealousy between the wives and mothers, and the husbands aren't comfortable either. Everybody winds up suffering.

Named for the region just south of Bamako from which it originated, it is a music based on a long tradition of dances and rhythms, and in its modern development has been dominated by female singers. "Our rhythms are very ancient, and the way we [play them] is traditional," Sangare says. "Sure, the bass guitars and other instruments are new things, but the rhythms are ancient." The music combines the *djembe* drum and *karinyang* ("scraper") with the jittery yet funky sound of the *kamalengoni* (six-stringed "young man's harp"). This latter instrument is a version of the traditional *donsongoni*, or forest hunter's harp, adapted by young people for their own music. It, and the Wassoulou style Sangare has brought to the world, symbolize youth and a sense of freedom. "I will fight until my dying day," Sangare has said, "for the rights of African women and of women throughout the world."

Ravi Shankar

Guitarist John McLaughlin once asked an Indian musician friend for Ravi Shankar's address. He was told to simply write, "Ravi Shankar, India." McLaughlin was incredulous. India has a population of more than 800 million people. But he sent the letter as instructed, and sure enough, in a while came a reply from the master sitarist.

No one has done more to popularize Indian music than Ravi Shankar. In the early part of this century, it was virtually unknown outside of India, except to members of the British Raj. Yet India's classical music has a history as long and rich as Europe's. Passed down orally from master to student, it goes back to the time of Bach, and is equally complex in structure and form. But it also departs considerably from Western classical music—there is a significant amount of freedom to improvise, and a great emphasis on rhythm. Shankar continues to perform great works of Hindustani classical music for audiences around the world, while at the same time working with pop groups and jazz musicians, constantly experimenting with new musical fusions.

Born in Benares, considered the holiest Hindu city in India, Shankar grew up with the Ganges in his backyard. His

He told me, 'If you want to learn properly, you have to leave all the glittery glamour of this Western world and come to me in my little village where I am living and stay there, and only then will I teach you properly.'

was a family of artists, and he began touring as a dancer and musician with his older brother's Uday Shankar Company at an early age. In 1932, at the age of twelve, Shankar joined his brother and traveled to Paris. The company was the first Indian troupe to tour internationally. It was a big production, managed and promoted by impresario Sol Hurok, whose other major act was the Anna Pavlova Ballet. "The whole ballet was working and creating new dances under my brother's direction," Shankar recalled when I first met him in 1988. "Costumes were being made, hundreds of yards of colorful brocade and different headdresses and ornaments. Then all the musical instruments my brother had collected—150 different varieties, all originally Indian, mostly folk, and lots of classical instruments. For the next few years I grew up in that atmosphere of dance and music. In Paris, I was put into school for about a year and a half, but that eventually ended. I was taught English, mathematics, and things like that. But it was dance and music that I lived."

Photographs of the company depict the young Ravi Shankar as a dandy, quite pleased with himself and obviously enjoying the good life as he traveled around the world first-class aboard the art nouveau jewel of the French Line, the SS *Normandie*. Tours took him not only to Paris but to New York and other cultural meccas, where the young musician met and mingled with many of the great artists of the time.

The sybaritic life didn't last forever. During the early phases of World War II, Shankar met his musical guru, Baba Allaudin Khan, a teacher who shaped the course of the rest of his life. Khan saw real talent but, Shankar recalls, "He told me, 'What you're doing is stupid. You're not concentrating on one thing, you're doing too many things . . . if you want to learn properly, you have to leave all the glittery glamour of this Western world and come to me in my little village where I am living and stay there, and only then will I teach you properly.' But I couldn't leave immediately. I was getting more famous as a dancer and becoming a young man and enjoying myself. But after some time I felt a tremendous emptiness, and I knew that music was the one thing that I wanted to do."

The training Shankar received from Khan was intense and grueling, and changed his lifestyle enormously. "After all the best hotels I had to go stay in a little room. The heat, the cockroaches, mosquitoes, flies, scorpions, the snakes all around, and the hard, coarse bed. So it was a torture for me in a way, physically and also mentally. I used to miss so many wonderful things that I had tasted in my life. It took me almost a year to get past that. But then, under his wonderful, strict but loving guidance, I stayed there for almost seven-and-a-half years, and worked up to fourteen hours a day. It was a completely different life, and I'm glad that I chose that life."

In the 1971 film about Ravi Shankar, *Raga*, there is a scene in which the artist returns to India to visit his guru, then more than 100 years old. Upon seeing him, Shankar prostrates himself and kisses his feet in reverence and adoration. It is difficult to imagine such an intense practice of discipleship and devotion in the West. Yet it has been a normal practice in the East for centuries. Shankar's daughter, Anoushka, is now his student. And while her apprenticeship is not as rigid as Shankar's was (she also attends high school in Encinitas, California), she is a serious professional who has toured worldwide with her famous father.

During the 1960s, Shankar taught many famous figures, including John Coltrane. Shankar recalls the great musician fondly: "He was a wonderful person. I always remember him. It's a pity that he died so young. He had so much to give. He was one person who was not copying our music but was trying to take the soul of it, or the inner feeling, which was rather unusual." Coltrane came to study with Shankar in search of the freedom inherent in modal improvisation, which frees the soloist from the constraints of chord structure. In addition to his desire to liberate himself from Western harmonic structures, Coltrane also saw music as a healing force and a means of approaching the divine, concepts found in much Indian and Sufi music.

It was Shankar's association with George Harrison and the Beatles, however, that drew the most attention, as well as misconceptions. "It brought all the young people to our music," Shankar says. "Of course it was a fad, very superficial. That's the negative side of it, and the drugs and all that sort of thing. On the other hand, I think what came out of it was good. There were some who stayed out of all that and showed much more respect for our music. They understood much more, and they are the best listeners today."

Shankar still performs regularly, and his playing is as elegant and powerful as ever. I

last saw him in 1997, performing with tabla virtuoso Zakir Hussain, the son of Shankar's earlier tabla accompanist, Alla Rakha. At the end of each complex rhythmic cycle, Shankar, who plays seated in a lotus position, would throw his head back, swooning with pleasure, and smile at Hussain, who, like Shankar, is mesmerizing to watch. I thought then how sensual and rhapsodic this great music is, how graceful in comparison to the stiffer classical styles of Europe. I thought of the similar sensuality I've seen in representations of Hindu gods. And I thought of how fortunate we have been to have such a great master in our midst.

Mercedes Sosa

Mercedes Sosa is a giant of the *nueva canción*, the "new song" movement that began in Argentina and Chile in the 1960s. Decidedly political, nueva canción is a music of protest and compassion—a commitment to fighting inequality and improving the lives of the majority. Along with Violetta Parra and the late Atahualpa Yupanqui, Sosa was a leader of the movement, which was stifled throughout South America after the CIA-sponsored coup that toppled Chile's Salvador Allende in 1973. She sang songs that encouraged agrarian reform, human rights, and democracy—songs that threatened the military regime then in power, and led to her exile from Argentina.

I didn't know all of this when I first put the needle down on her riveting version of the Violetta Parra classic, "Gracias a la Vida." I was moved by the simple beauty of her voice: soft, deep, and compelling. In the background, I could hear the sound of a crowd of thousands erupting into applause. My Spanish wasn't great, but I didn't need a translator to understand what had happened onstage that night in February 1982, when she returned from exile to a country in transition toward democracy. Years later, in 1987, Mercedes

Exile is really, like the Greeks said, the most severe punishment you can make a person suffer. A popular singer has to be very strong to stand being so far from the things she sings about.

Sosa sat before me in the radio studio. I looked across the control board at the stout, shy woman—now a grandmother—and wondered what her life had been like.

Sosa describes a pleasant childhood, surrounded by a large supportive family. She grew up in Tucumán, an area of northwestern Argentina known as "the garden of the Republic." She describes it as both a city and the smallest province in Argentina. "I didn't just grow up in the city," she said, "but also near nature, trees—things that greatly influence a person's life."

From a young age, people told Sosa that she had a lovely voice; when she was fifteen she won an amateur competition at a radio station. Becoming a famous singer, however, was not something she predicted or even particularly desired. "I didn't like to sing in public," she said. "I am enormously timid, so much so that when I get on stage it takes me three or four songs to overcome it. I've spent my whole life trying to overcome this timidness, to be able to communicate with people, or at least enjoy what I'm singing. The people have guided me to the place of popularity I now occupy. But I never wanted to be a singer, either in Tucumán or anywhere else."

While she has grown comfortable singing for friends, onstage and off, Sosa has never gotten used to the life of "hotels, planes, and tours." The price of fame, she has learned, can be high, especially if you're dubbed a "protest" singer living under a hostile military regime. The government effectively put an end to her career by arresting her during a concert in 1975, then threatening her with death. "I had to leave in 1979," she said. "They took away all my work—radio, television, personal appearances. So I went to Madrid because of the common language." The move away from the country and the people she loved was made even more poignant and painful by her husband's death in 1978, just prior to her exile. "Everything happened at once," she said. "One can overcome all of these political things. What is very difficult to overcome is the death of loved ones, against which you can do nothing but wait until this great pain subsides."

Exile only deepened her mourning. "Exile is really, like the Greeks said, the most severe punishment you can make a person suffer," she admits. "A popular singer has to be very strong to stand being so far from the things she sings about." But while she suffered a great deal, the experience of exile in Europe also gave her style an added depth, which she eventually brought back to Argentina, along with an international reputation.

Sosa has been dubbed "the voice of the silent majority." It is a responsibility she readily accepts, but qualifies. "For many years," she says. "I've known that I have a responsibility to sing for people all over the world, for those who supported me and helped me all my life. . . . The songs have changed over time, from songs of struggle and of barricades to songs that speak more of the anguish of every human being. When I returned to

Argentina in 1982, I had to find a new way to express myself onstage to my people, to give them the encouragement to continue, because the struggle to live in Argentina and in Latin America is hard enough. I didn't want to create more problems for them, but to show them new energy."

Sosa admits that she has changed over the years. Indeed, she encourages change. When people note her apparent migration away from political issues, she says, "I don't think there's such a radical change . . . It's another way of singing, which has opened many roads all over the world, so that I can talk to people about whatever I want."

A powerful matriarchal figure, Sosa is a survivor who relies heavily on the support and encouragement of her many friendships. Her experiences resonate in her rich, distinctive voice, expressing the hopes and dreams not just of the people of Argentina, but of millions everywhere.

Atahualpa Yupanqui

On a night in late May 1992, European viewers watching the Barcelona European Cup victory celebrations on television were startled when the networks interrupted the broadcast with a bulletin announcing the death of Atahualpa Yupanqui. The broad and noble face, familiar from the covers of his many record albums and books of poetry and prose, flashed across television screens in Spain and France. Yupanqui had died in his hotel room in Nimes, France, where he was the guest of honor at the 1992 Cartelera festival of Spanish films. His death, at eighty-three, cast a pall over the festival, attended by thousands of devoted fans who had come to hear him perform his adored songs.

Atahualpa Yupanqui is known as the father of *nueva canción*, a music of protest and compassion that emphasized indigenous culture and humanitarian values in the face of dictatorships such as those in Chile and in Yupanqui's native Argentina. He was born Hector Roberto Chavero Uramburu in Pergamino, Argentina, in 1908, to an Amerindian father and a Basque mother. He later changed his name to Atahualpa (the last Incan ruler) Yupanqui (an honorary title given to Quechua warriors). He learned to play violin, then guitar, eventually studying with Bautista Almiron, a famous Argentine guitar teacher.

As a young man, Yupanqui rode horseback across the pampas, exploring Argentina as an itinerant musician when much of the country was still untouched by the automobile. "There," he once said, "the mysteries of nature are so overwhelming that music comes as a support, a comforting echo we murmur to ourselves." He landed in Buenos Aires in 1926, but did not find success there. He sang songs he had written or discovered during his horseback travels, and the sophisticated *porteños* judged him provincial. Yupanqui left Buenos Aires and traveled throughout South America, learning local musical traditions and folklore and incorporating them into his music in songs that were to become famous everywhere: "Aires Indios," "Soy Libre, Soy Bueno," "Duerme Negrito," "Trabajo, Quiero Trabajo," and dozens of others. In these songs, he sang out simply and eloquently against the injustices he saw during his travels, in a sonorous, haunting voice that was nevertheless somehow strangely comforting. His legend began to spread across Argentina and throughout Latin America.

Yupanqui achieved worldwide renown in 1948 following his arrival in Paris, where he debuted as the opening act for a young French singer named Edith Piaf at the Olympia Theater. In Europe, Yupanqui became friends with Picasso, Luis Buñuel, Paul Eluard, and Piaf, who introduced him to Parisian musical circles. In 1949, Yupanqui gave more than sixty concerts throughout Europe, and his fame was assured. For his elegantly simple yet profound songs, he was twice awarded the prestigious Académie Charles Gros Award, first in 1950 and again in 1969.

Yupanqui inspired a generation of nueva canción singers, including Mercedes Sosa, Victor

Jarra (who was murdered by soldiers during the 1973 CIA-sponsored coup that killed Chilean President Salvador Allende and put Pinochet into power), Violetta Parra, Silvio Rodríguez, Pablo Milanes, and Milton Nascimento. He was also a literary giant, writing poems and prose about the earth, the wind on the pampas, the human relation to the natural world, and the plight of poor country people trying to survive in big cities. His writing in all forms led artists to become engaged in the struggle for human rights, showing in his soft-spoken way that music can make a difference in lands where guns, dictators, and brutality are the order of the day.

Sun Ra

Sun Ra, a.k.a. Le Sun, Le Solar Ra, Le Sony'r Ra, claimed that he had visited the planet Saturn. The visit changed his life. And indeed, his often bizarre-sounding music and his flamboyant persona can seem otherworldly. He produced 120 records on his own independent El Saturn label and dozens of others for record companies around the world. He was prodigious, especially for someone completely outside of mainstream jazz and the avant-garde jazz coterie. He made many recordings for ESP, a label that also produced albums by Timothy Leary, the Fugs, and Albert Ayler. Sun Ra's 1966 ESP release, *The Heliocentric Worlds of Sun Ra*, was illustrated with an image of Sun Ra next to the great cosmologists with whom he felt kinship: Kepler, Copernicus, and Galileo. The text on the album was printed in Esperanto.

While some of Sun Ra's music was out there, especially his piano solos, many of his big band arrangements and performances were as earthly as any classic Kansas City swing from the 1940s and embraced the great traditions in American music. For his young fans in the 1960s, like me and my high school surfing buddies, he was a mysterious character

> [Music] is all I have in the world, being motherless, father-less, and friendless, too, for that matter. Unfortunately, I have learned not to trust people. I am a little afraid of normal people. Their greatest desire in life seems to be to maim and destroy either themselves or others.

akin to something from a Marvel Comic. When I finally saw him in concert, he met all of my expectations. Jay Green, a visionary impresario, brought Sun Ra's Solar Arkestra to a dilapidated Art Deco palace called Myron's Ballroom. Some band members were suspended from tracks in the ceiling and moved back and forth like astronauts. Others were arrayed in heavy gold lamé, turbans, helmets, and burnooses. Sun Ra wore a space helmet with Egyptian motifs and played on strange instruments that looked like chambered nautiluses. Jazz hounds, punks, and avant-gardists of all stripes turned out for this one.

Sun Ra had given theatrical performances like this for years. His spaceship motifs and charismatic fashion statements were harbingers of musicians of the 1970s and 1980s such as George Clinton and Bootsy Collins's Parliament-Funkadelic. ("This boy was definitely out to lunch," George Clinton told the *Toronto Sun* in 1979, "the same place I eat at!" The liner notes of Parliament-Funkadelic's 1974 album *Standing on the Verge of Gettin' It On* listed Jimi Hendrix, Sly Stone, and Sun Ra as the group's biggest influences.) Sun Ra used elements of theater to get his music and philosophy across with a sense of fun. As his biographer, John F. Szwed, writes in *Space is the Place*, "It was the expressivity of music and its effect on listeners which concerned him most of all." When asked how he thought his music helped people, Sun Ra replied,

"First of all I express sincerity. There is also that sense of humor, by which people sometimes learn to laugh about themselves. I mean, the situation is so serious that the people could go crazy because of it. They need to smile and realize how ridiculous everything is. A race without a sense of humor is in bad shape. A race needs clowns. In earlier days people knew that. Kings always had a court jester around. In that way he was always reminded how ridiculous things are. I believe that nations should have jesters too, in the Congress, near the President, everywhere . . . You could call me the jester of the Creator. The whole world, all the disease and misery, it's all ridiculous." If he saw himself as a sort of cosmic jester, he took the job seriously.

Sun Ra was born Herman Sonny Blount in Birmingham, Alabama, on May 22, 1914. He was by all accounts a special child, very bright and inquisitive, and enjoyed spending time alone. The civil rights movement wasn't to begin for another thirty years, and growing up in bitterly segregated Birmingham was difficult. I asked him how he got started in music. "I felt guided my whole so-called lifetime to do what I'm doing," he said. "I never intended to be a musician. I wasn't interested in music. I was mostly interested in being a scholar. And then I came home one day, eleven years old, and there was a piano for a birthday present. I hadn't taken any lessons. But I sat down and played. A friend said I was playing by ear."

camp in Pennsylvania. The Army psychiatrist judged him "a psychopathic personality." "[Music] is all I have in the world," Sun Ra said at the time, quoted in *Space is the Place*, "being motherless, fatherless, and friendless, too, for that matter. Unfortunately, I have learned not to trust people. I am a little afraid of normal people. Their greatest desire in life seems to be to maim and destroy either themselves or others."

In 1946 Sun Ra moved to the jazz haven of Chicago, where he became a pianist with the Fletcher Henderson orchestra at Club Delisa. He stayed with Henderson nearly eighteen months, writing arrangements and playing every night except Monday. Sun Ra is remembered as an anomaly during his Chicago days. A non-smoking, nondrinking, and apparently celibate musician was unusual enough, but discussing physics, astronomy, and space travel was downright eccentric. There he formed his Arkestra, a band that would stay with him for forty years until his death in 1993. He next went to Montreal and then to New York, where the Arkestra played and recorded for many years. In 1968, Sun Ra finally settled in Philadelphia.

The family of musicians variously called The Solar Arkestra, Space Arkestra, and the Intergalactic Myth-Science Arkestra lived together in a Philadelphia commune and were committed to a lifetime relationship with the organization. Sun Ra demanded that music be their life. "You eat it, breathe it, live it," he said. He was their spiritual advisor as well as their bandleader.

Sun Ra was an avid reader, with a keen interest in philosophy, theology, and history. He saw himself primarily as a scholar. "I love to read, be alone, study, research. But I have to present what was learned from another dimension, what I have to offer to people. The music speaks about other things, and all those things are impossible."

Sun Ra was especially interested in Egyptology and spent a lot of time during his

Within a year, Sun Ra was composing music. He led his own band while still in his teens. He also became interested in scientific writings as well as in religion and mysticism. He attended music classes at Huntsville, Alabama, then went to Florida A & M, where he received his diploma. During World War II, he registered as a conscientious objector and was imprisoned briefly, then sent to a work

Chicago days studying revisionist histories of Egypt and Africa. It was then that he changed his name to Le Sony'r Ra, Ra being the feminine form of Re, the sun god of ancient Egypt. Eventually he used the abbreviated form Sun Ra, which he considered his *nom des affaires*. I had heard a lot of things about his visit to the great pyramid at Giza. "Something is very different there," he told me. "The sun shines differently. In fact, I could feel it going all the way through me and shining out my back. I went up into the king's chamber with four fellows in the band. 'This pyramid is good for the name Ra,' I told them, 'and his name hasn't been said in this room for a long time. Let's say it nine times.' So we said 'Ra' nine times. And all the lights went out. We had to walk down the ramp backward. We couldn't get out of the pyramid, so we stooped down, went through a tunnel to the queen's chamber. And the lights came on. When I came back to New York, a person came up and laid a book on the piano, and in the book it said the queen's chamber is a place of enlightenment."

Sun Ra spoke often about his mission as a musician, a seeker of wisdom, and an intergalactic explorer. He saw his works as cosmic dramas meant to enlighten and entertain. "I paint pictures of infinity with my music," he once said, "and that's why a lot of people can't understand it. My intergalactic music concerns the music of the galaxies, intergalactic thought and travel." During his performances he spoke of the dangers of the arms race, the spectre of nuclear holocaust, and the need to create an alternate future.

Sun Ra's otherworldliness was a response to a real world he understood all too well. He himself always put it best. To quote him again from *Space is the Place*: "I've never been part of the planet. I've been isolated [since I was] a child away from it. Right in the midst

of everything and not being a part of it. Them troubles peoples got, prejudices and all that, I didn't know a thing about it, until I got to be about fourteen years old. It was as if I was somewhere else that imprinted this purity on my mind, another kind of world. That is my music playing the kind of world I know about. It's like someone else from another planet trying to find out what to do. That's the kind of mind or spirit I have, it's not programmed—from the family, the church, from the schools, from the government. I don't have a programmed mind. I know what they're talking about, but they don't know what I'm talking about. I'm in the midst of what they're doing but they have never been in the midst of what has been impressed upon my mind as being a pure solar world."

Caetano Veloso

Caetano Veloso is the most popular singer to have emerged from the talented group of MPB (*música popular brasileira*) artists in the late 1960s. A philosophy student who read Sartre and Heidegger and who at first wanted to be a film-maker, Veloso was controversial from the beginning. Along with Gilberto Gil, he was booed from the stage in 1968 for playing electric guitar and wearing plastic clothing. Later, he was forced into exile by the military dictatorship, and spent several years immersed in the musical atmosphere of London. There, his already eclectic musical brew was infused with even more diverse elements.

Lately, Veloso has been performing on film soundtracks and singing classic Latin American songs in Spanish. Onstage, he dresses in classic suits, a distinguished-looking man of 54. It's difficult to imagine him today as he was in 1968, in plastic clothing, confronting audiences for their insularity with the manifesto *E Proibir Proibido* (It's Forbidden to Forbid), a slogan he borrowed from the general strike in France of that May.

Veloso was born and raised in Santo Amaro de Purificação, a small town not far from Salvador and Bahia, the center of

Although we are a very poor country, we have quite a rich tradition of popular music. It surpasses even the American tradition. It's varied, creative, courageous, inventive. Brazilian pop music is quite heroic.

Afro-Brazilian culture. He now lives in Bahia, and talks fondly about the rich cultural mix that distinguishes his homeland. "Brazil began in Bahia," he says. "The Portuguese arrived in Bahia, and Salvador was the capital of the country during the entire colonial period. It changed to Rio only when the royal family came from Portugal and brought the court and the center of their empire to Brazil. Before all this happened, Bahia was the most important part of the country. The majority of black slaves were brought to Bahia. And the majority of blacks still live here. Bahia has always been more African, numerically, than any other part of Brazil. It's very Portuguese architecturally, and very African musically, and the population is quite dark. Not black—half black. Like me."

The African influence in Bahia is perhaps most noticeable in its unique rendition of *carnaval*. "Carnaval in Brazil has always meant a lot," Veloso says. "Not only in Rio, Recife, and in Bahia, but all over Brazil. In Bahia, it has grown in a different way because it's more African, it's more rock 'n roll, it's more pop, it's more now. From the sixties on, Bahia has adapted the carnaval to the new reality of the city and of the world, and this has made carnaval in Bahia . . . somehow stronger than anywhere else in Brazil."

Veloso's own work is also defined by similar flair and originality. He began composing songs in 1964, when he was studying philosophy. While it became clear early on that music would be his true calling, Veloso's eclectic interests have proven useful in his endeavors.

Today he directs his own music videos, and his background in philosophy inspires his thinking and his lyrics, which have earned him a reputation in the Portuguese-speaking world as a great writer as well as a great musician.

Veloso's songs were first popularized by his younger sister, Maria Bethania, an important Brazilian singer in her own right. His own notoriety, however, came with *Tropicalia*, an album he recorded with Gilberto Gil in 1968. Fusing Brazilian music with English and American rock, the album put a new twist on MPB. It was criticized for the electronic instruments and foreign sounds it brought into the MPB tradition. In fact, the media attacked the two for being "unpatriotic," and purists went so far as to boo them off stage. The music, however, spoke strongly to a younger generation of Brazilians, disillusioned by the dictatorship and eager to flout convention.

Unlike many artists who emerged from Brazil in the 1960s, Veloso, along with Gilberto Gil, is still hugely popular with young audiences, and his music continues to resonate with their lives. After the generals fell from power and censorship was lifted, many people didn't want to hear more songs about pretty women and nice beaches. Finally able to express themselves freely, young artists wrote songs critical of the church, the police, and the government. Reggae, punk, and other socially conscious musical forms took precedence. Veloso's popularity, however, never waned. I wondered if he made a special effort to communicate with Brazil's youth. "I don't

> I do think music makes some things move and creates differences. But it's very difficult to be conscious of what kind of differences it can make.

make any effort," he says. "I just work hard because I feel like doing things. I think a lot and pay attention to what's going on. There is something that connects me and Gil with youth—as a subject of discussion, our ideas are still being presented. It's not like people only remember what we did, it's how our conversation with these young people is now."

That connection, however, was not achieved without suffering. Both Veloso and Gil were put in prison, then forced into exile by the dictatorship that ruled Brazil from 1963 to 1985. He says he'll never forget how the federal police quickly organized his documents and put him on a plane. "We were not sure of our final destination before we left Brazil," he recalls. Flying from Rio to Lisbon, then later to Paris, he finally settled in London.

Adjusting to life in another country was not easy. "London felt dark," he says, "and I felt far away from myself. But then we started playing music. Ralph Mace [from] Famous Records liked what he heard and wanted me and Gilberto Gil to make a record. And so we did. In fact, Gil did one and I did two. Working made me feel a little better. But when it was possible to return to Brazil in 1972, I immediately came back."

Few artists have been as consistently and prodigiously creative as Veloso and Gilberto Gil. When I asked Veloso to explain the longevity of so many Brazilian musicians, he had this to say: "Although we are a very poor country, we have quite a rich tradition of popular music. It surpasses even the American tradition. It's varied, creative, courageous, inven-

tive. Brazilian pop music is quite heroic."

Now in his fifties, Veloso has seen his country go through great political and social upheavals. But despite his own personal rebellions and his revolutionary musical style, he is reluctant to link music directly with social change. "I do think music makes some things move and creates differences," he says. "But it's very difficult to be conscious of what kind of differences it can make."

The Latin American songs on a recent recording, *Fina Estampa*, are slow, dreamy, and very romantic versions of classics that Veloso sings in Spanish. He wanted to evoke the sentimental quality of the Brazilian songs of his childhood. "I also wanted to make them very personal," he says, "and very Brazilian in the way that they're all filtered through bossa nova and *tropicalismo*. 'Fina Estampa' has bossa nova's anti-macho approach to sentiment. And it has tropicalist humor in all of the interpretations and arrangements. It's very subtle, but it's there. My approach, in the João Gilberto tradition, is a delicate way of conceiving chords and tempos and the way you use your voice. It creates a big contrast with the tradition of Mexicans or Argentineans who sing tangos or boleros or rancheras. You know, it's strangely too cool and strangely not macho enough for the material."

Veloso's soft, smooth voice is his trademark, and he acknowledges that his greatest debt is to João Gilberto, the alpha and omega of bossa nova. "He's a master," Veloso says. "For me he's the center of the reality of popular music in Brazil, past, present, and future."

Baden Powell

I first heard Baden Powell in the late 1960s on an import album called *Apaixanado*. I had no doubt heard him before—a fine song of his, "Samba de Bençao" (Samba of Blessing), was used in the 1966 Claude Lelouch film *A Man and a Woman*. Here was popular guitar playing with classical finesse, the drive of good jazz, the soul

of great world music, and a good measure of the unexpected. It sounded like a great master playing acoustic guitar with very thick strings, plucking them harder than anyone I'd ever heard. It was music of great subtlety and complexity, but delivered with guts, especially on that bass string, the bottom end.

I've collected many of Powell's recordings. He has become a sort of mythic figure for me. Born in 1937 in Varre-e-Sai, a small town in the Rio de Janeiro state, Powell was named by his father

after the founder of the Boy Scouts. He became famous among the first wave of bossa nova pioneers, working with Antonio Carlos Jobim, Vinícius de Moraes, and others. He left Brazil in the late 1960s during the years of the dictatorship, and spent the next twenty years in Europe. He returned to Brazil in 1989.

I have never seen Powell perform, and to my knowledge he has given only a handful of concerts in the U.S. But I've heard him mesmerize crowds on live recordings, doing things that make it sound as if two guitarists are playing. He has incredibly nimble fingers, great chord progressions, and a rhythmic drive that derives from Afro-Brazilian traditions. Together with Vinícius, Powell researched traditional Bahian music and incorporated it into his own, which accounts at least partly for its unusual edge.

There are no guitarists like Brazilian guitarists. Their wildly inventive chord progressions bring constant surprise and inspire guitar players everywhere. When Pat Metheny went to Brazil and heard Baden Powell and Toninho Horta, he was completely astounded.

Powell remains a somewhat obscure figure. Music encyclopedias rarely mention him. But for me, his exquisite and powerful art will always remain as unique in Brazilian music as his name.

Tom Waits

Tom Waits, born in 1949 in Pomona, California, is one of America's most gifted lyricists and singers. His art is a union of opposites: His voice is both rough and smooth, his lyrics sentimental and hard-nosed. His voice may be gravelly ("I just had it lowered," he once quipped to David Letterman), but his pitch is dead on. "Well, you know, I can sing like Pavarotti if I want to," he said when I interviewed him in 1992, "but I find that I feel more comfortable the way I do it." His sound is often fractured and contentious, though his ballads are moving. His songwriting style, with its painterly imagery and original metaphors, defies categorization. Yet he is quintessentially American, a real folk hero. He is an iconoclastic presence in American pop, with a stylistic range from punk to Irving Berlin.

Waits has continually reinvented himself. His albums do not arrive on any sort of regular basis; we sometimes have to wait years. He started in the 1970s working with fine jazz studio musicians, living out of his car, hanging out with Rickie Lee Jones. He later brought in musicians like guitarist Marc Ribot, who helped Waits deconstruct his musical style, creating a more Captain Beefheart sound. "I love Captain Beefheart," Waits says. "He's a true innovator. He has a mad quality; he takes things that fell off a truck and adapts them. "

Waits has also forged an interesting acting career. He performed a long run of Frank's Wild Years at Chicago's Steppenwolf Theater. He has appeared in such films as Francis Ford Coppola's *Bram Stoker's Dracula* (1992), Robert Altman's *Short Cuts* (1993), for which he received laudatory reviews, and perhaps most notably Jim Jarmusch's *Down By Law* (1986). "Jarmusch is a very good friend," Waits says. "We have a rapport. He's Dr. Sullen, and we work real well together. He's a great observer of human nature and loves the details. I'm big on details, so it's great to work with somebody you have that shorthand with."

In the early '70s, Waits was performing at the Troubadour when he was spotted by Herb Cohen, an influential manager who secured the artist a deal with Irving Azoff's Asylum label. His debut record, the wistful *Closing Time*, appeared in 1973, followed by *The Heart of Saturday Night*, which featured scenes and characters drawn from the realm of the ordinary: working men, waitresses, assorted drifters. Waits's third album, *Nighthawks at the Diner* (1976), took its title from the Edward Hopper painting reproduced on the jacket cover. Here Waits's songs were a musical counterpart to Hopper's painting; both artists brilliantly captured blue-collar, street-level life in America, though Waits did so with a heavy dose of humor and sympathy.

Waits left Asylum Records in 1983 and signed with Island. The rough, edgy sound of his debut Island album, *Swordfishtrombones*, signaled a musical departure for him.

Subsequent albums, like *Rain Dogs* and *Big Time,* had a similarly fractured feel and were full of new sounds: toy instruments, mega-phones—a blend of Beefheart, Harry Partch, and a measure of dada. These were very different from the earlier jazz-based albums, and the voice had become rougher than ever.

In 1993, Waits released *The Black Rider*, an album of songs from a stage production directed by Robert Wilson and written by William S. Burroughs. The production also featured Waits in an acting role. His latest collection, *Beautiful Maladies* (1998), is a compilation of previous Island releases. His last studio album of new material, however, *Bone Machine*, released in 1992, is a raw, stripped down, percussive, and wonderfully energetic album. When I interviewed Waits, *Bone Machine* had just been released. Karen Schoemer of the *New York Times* said this about it: "The whole album crackles and hisses as if coming out of a transistor radio. But expressly because so much of the glamour has been stripped away, *Bone Machine* has an unconditional purity that is nothing short of breathtaking." The recording made many critics' top-ten lists that year and it went on to win a Grammy for best alternative album.

Bone Machine was to have been recorded in a studio, but Waits chose a bare room instead. "I've come more and more to the point where I think the sound is married to the music," he says. "We recorded this thing in a shed, you know, a real shed. It was great. The first day of recording was difficult because we were booked into this room. And I said, 'Oh, man, this room sounds terrible.' I was a little embarrassed. So was everybody else. But then I found a little storage room, and I said, 'Well, boy, this room sounds pretty good, so let's do it down here.' And everybody looked at me like, 'Down here, well, geez, this room's not really a studio.'"

This reminded me of listening to blues records produced by Marshall Chess in

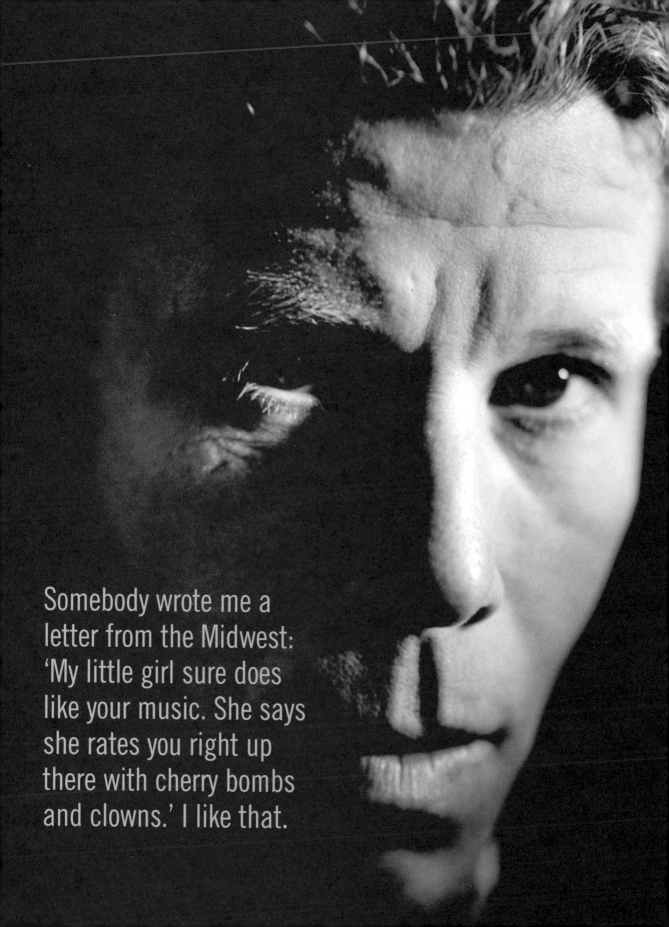

Somebody wrote me a letter from the Midwest: 'My little girl sure does like your music. She says she rates you right up there with cherry bombs and clowns.' I like that.

Some nights [being on the road] is like getting skinned and dipped in lemon juice, and other nights it's like you're eight miles high and, you know, the world is covered with mattresses and you can't get hurt.

Chicago in the '50s. You can hear all of the raw energy of the original session. Waits agreed. "Hey, if it sounds good, you do it. I'm at the point where I like letting the world in. We had a broken window with a sheet over it, and a door with a squeaky hinge with no lock on it, and a cement floor, and a water heater in the corner . . . I love letting the world into the studio, rather than trying to shut it out."

I asked Waits, whom I've always perceived as hypersensitive, if it was nerve-wracking to go on the road after the release of an album. "The road is always rough 'cause it's different every night. I mean, that's why you do it. Some nights it's like getting skinned and dipped in lemon juice, and other nights it's like you're eight miles high and, you know, the world is covered with mattresses and you can't get hurt. You just have to be ready for the highs and the lows of it."

Waits lives in "a little town out in the sticks" in northern California with his wife, writer Kathleen Brennan, and their two children. I wanted to know if being a family man has changed his outlook. "I think I'm getting wilder in a way, so, gee, I don't know. I mean, my kids are very musical. Kids write thousands of songs before they even learn to talk. They write the best songs, better than anybody I know, because they don't know what they're doing; they just fall into it. They also make up words all the time, which I like, 'cause I'm big on words. It's usually the sound of the word that I'm attracted to, especially in a song. They have to be like *sound items.* Every word

has its own resonance and its own shape, its own things that it does. Somebody wrote me a letter from the Midwest: 'My little girl sure does like your music. She says she rates you right up there with cherry bombs and clowns.' I like that."

Which comes first for him, the words and poetry or the music? "I don't know," he says. "It's always all mixed up together. You gotta start somewhere. We like to start writing in a room with a very crummy tape recorder, a pawn shop tape recorder. The sound we get on the tape recorder is really alive, and then we have to go into the studio and see if we can find the same world, the same sound-world. I'm also interested in alternative sound sources. More and more I'm exploring things that aren't necessarily instruments but sound great. When you're writing in a room where there's nothing, you'll turn something into an instrument . . . I like things that have struggle involved, particularly with percussion. I think drums play a lot better when you're mad. Unfamiliarity is good for the development of the mystery of musicianship; it's important to keep that alive. What I like to do with the band is say, 'Well, let's try this thing once, all together, and now let's switch instruments, let's everybody just give your instrument to somebody else, and let's get really off balance here and see if we can play it again with no coordinates and no center of gravity.' I like to work with people who respond to those things."

Our conversation turned to avant-garde composer Harry Partch. "He was always hitting something that wasn't really an instrument," Waits recalled. "But all the instruments that we know, had to go through this evolution. There's skin and metal and wood and glass and wind. Basically, you're dealing with the same physics that they were dealing with then, but the world is changing and people are finding that there are a lot of recyclable items that are fascinating sound sources."

I told Waits a story about jazz violinist Joe Venuti. He once pushed a piano out of a fifth-floor window to see what the piano's major tonic would be when it hit the pavement. "Hey, everybody who plays the piano wants to see a piano thrown off a building," Waits says. "That's the dream. 'Cause they're so heavy, and you always have to go to them. I think everybody who plays the piano wants to see it smash on the rocks."

Waits explains his move from the smooth jazzy sound of his earlier recordings to something more primitive as part of a search. "You're always looking for something that feels new," he says. "I'm just trying to go a little bit outside of myself, which is where your best work comes from, when you're off balance. I'm always exploring a little bit at a time in the studio. You want to hear something you've never heard before; we've integrated some farm machinery into this record."

When singing alone at a piano, Waits can be extremely moving. His encores are often ballads. He enjoys playing the whiskey-soaked saloon singer; it's usually late, and the place is empty except for him and the bartender. There's a nice interplay in Waits's concerts between the ballads and the newer songs. "I go back and forth," he says. "I like to hear family heirlooms thrown against the wall; I like a lot of different sounds. But the other side of me is the old drunk in the corner who had too much wine and is starting to get a little sentimental."

There is biblical imagery in some of Waits's songs, particularly *Bone Machine*'s "The Earth Died Screaming." "It's my wife's fault," Waits

says. "She's a lapsed Catholic. That song is from the book of Rudy, actually—one of the lost books of the Bible. He was one of the disciples. He was in, then he was out, then he was in. He finally opened up a café."

Waits loves great old gospel music. I figured he might have some admiration for street preachers, too. He does. "I used to hear 'em all the time in downtown L.A.," he recalls, "those guys with their own sound systems and microphones and briefcases. They'd always pick, like, five o'clock when it was really busy. They were usually singing like it was the most important thing going on, but it was disregarded by everyone. It used to make me really sad; I would always stop and listen, 'cause, you know, when you have something to say that's important to you and no one's listening, it's a lonely place. It takes a lot of courage and conviction. Sometimes it elevates you knowing nobody's listening; there's a freedom in that too. I love those guys. Plus their sound systems—I love the sound of those little speakers."

Waits has a particular fondness for the last song on *Bone Machine*, "That Feel," written by Keith Richards. "Music follows him around," Waits says. "He's totally intuitive; he's got gypsy in him, and a little pirate. He's wild, like something in captivity. We wrote a lot of songs together. Making music with him is like getting on a ship and going far from home. He loves adventure and I love adventure. I played drums mostly when he wrote. I play upright bass on the song—that was one of those trades. And you can hear me coughing."

I always loved Waits's Vegas version of "Straight to the Top." He coughs on that one too. "Yeah," he says. "Everything is valid. That's my theory."

Selected Discography

Albita
Dicen Que . . . , 1996 (SONY MUSIC)
Una Mujer Como Yo, 1997 (SONY MUSIC)

Asha Bhosle
The Greatest Hits of Asha Bhosle, 1990 (MUSIC INDIA)
Golden Voices from the Silver Screen, 1990 (ACE)

Rubén Blades
Rubén Blades and Willie Colon, ¡Metiendo Mano!, 1977 (FANIA)
Rubén Blades y Seis Del Solar, Buscando America, 1984
    (ELEKTRA/ASYLUM)
La Rosa de los Vientos, 1996 (SONY MUSIC)

Camarón de la Isla
Flamenco Vivo, 1987 (POLYGRAM IBÉRICA)
Camarón with the Royal Philharmonic Orchestra, Soy Gitano,
    1989 (POLYGRAM IBÉRICA)
Autorretrato, 1990 (POLYGRAM IBÉRICA)
Camarón with Paco de Lucía, Potro de Rabia y Miel, 1992
    (POLYGRAM IBÉRICA)

Celia Cruz
Irrepetible, 1994 (RMM RECORDS & VIDEO)
Homenaje a los Santos, 1994 (POLYGRAM)
Celia Cruz with La Sonora Mantancera, 100% Azucar! The
    Best of . . ., 1997 (RHINO)
Celia's Duets, 1997 (RMM RECORDS & VIDEO)

Manu Dibango
Polysonik, 1990 (S.N.A.)
Wakafrika, 1994 (GIANT)
Manu Dibango with Cuarteto Patria, Cubafrica, 1998 (CELLULOID)

Djavan
Djavan, 1989 (DISCOS CBS)
Alumbramento and Djavan, 1992 (CAPITOL)
Malasia, 1996 (SONY MUSIC)

Brian Eno
Discreet Music, 1975 (EG)
Ambient 1: Music for Airports, 1978 (EG)
Brian Eno and David Byrne, My Life in the Bush of Ghosts,
    1981 (EG)
Nerve Net, 1992 (WARNER BROS.)

Cesaria Evora
Miss Perfumado, 1992 (LUSAFRICA); 1998 (NONESUCH)
Cesaria Evora, 1995 (NONESUCH)
Live à L'Olympia, 1996 (LUSAFRICA)
Cabo Verde, 1997 (LUSAFRICA)

Fela Anikulapo Kuti
Army Arrangement, 1984 (CELLULOID)
Fela Anikulapo Kuti and Egypt '80, Odoo, 1990 (SHANACHIE)
Music is the Weapon of the Future, 1998 (EXWORKS)

Djivan Gasparyan
I Will Not Be Sad In This World, 1989 (WARNER BROS.)
Apricots from Eden, 1996 (TRADITIONAL CROSSROADS)

Antonio Carlos Jobim
Terra Brasilis, 1980 (WARNER BROS.)
Compact Jazz: Antonio Carlos Jobim, 1990 (POLYGRAM)
Verve Jazz Masters Volume 13, 1994 (POLYGRAM)
The Man from Ipanema, 1995 (POLYGRAM)

Umm Kulthum
Tichouf Oumori, 1926–1935, no date (BUDA MUSIQUE)
Anthologie de la Musique Arabe: 1926 Volume 1, 1989 (CDV)

Salif Keita
Soro, 1987 (ISLAND/MANGO)
The Mansa Of Mali: A Retrospective, 1994 (ISLAND/MANGO)
Folon (The Past), 1995 (ISLAND/MANGO)
Salif Keita and Les Ambassadeurs, Seydou Bathily, 1997
    (SONODISC)

Khaled
N'ssi N'ssi, 1993 (BARCLAY)
Sahra, 1996 (BARCLAY)
Hafla Live, 1998 (BARCLAY)

Nusrat Fateh Ali Khan
Nusrat Fateh Ali Khan and Party, Devotional and Love Songs,
    1992 (REAL WORLD)
Nusrat Fateh Ali Khan with Michael Brook, Mustt Mustt, 1990
    (REAL WORLD)
Nusrat Fateh Ali Khan and Party, The Last Prophet, 1994
    (REAL WORLD)
Nusrat Fateh Ali Khan with Michael Brook, Night Song, 1995
    (REAL WORLD)

Baaba Maal

Lam Toro, 1992 (ISLAND/MANGO)
Firin' In Fouta, 1994 (ISLAND/MANGO)
Nomad Soul, 1998 (PALM PICTURES)

Madredeus

O Espírito da Paz, 1994 (CAPITOL)
Ainda (soundtrack from the film Lisbon Story), 1995 (CAPITOL)
Existir, 1997 (CAPITOL)
O Paraíso, 1997 (CAPITOL)

Lata Mangeshkar

Lata Mangeshkar and Jagjit Singh, Sajda, An Offering of
    Ghazals, 1991 (THE GRAMOPHONE COMPANY OF INDIA)

Bob Marley

Legend: The Best of Bob Marley and the Wailers, 1984 (ISLAND)
One Love, 1991 (POLI-RHYTHM)
Songs of Freedom (box set), 1992 (ISLAND)

Beny Moré

The Most from Beny Moré, 1990 (BMG)
Colección de Oro, 1991 (PHILIPS)
Y Hoy Como Ayer, 1992 (BMG)

Milton Nascimento

Clube da Esquina (2 vols.), 1971; remastered 1995 (EMI BRASIL)
Minas, 1975; remastered 1995 (EMI-ODEON BRASIL)
Anima, 1982 (VERVE)
Miltons, 1989 (VERVE)
Sentinela, 1989 (POLYGRAM DO BRASIL)

Youssou N'Dour

The Lion, 1989 (VIRGIN)
Set, 1990 (VIRGIN)
Lay Suma Lay, 1996 (STERN'S MUSIC)
The Guide (Wommat), 1994 (SONY MUSIC)

Astor Piazzolla

Astor Piazzolla and the New Tango Quintet, Tango: Zero Hour,
    1986 (AMERICAN CLAVÉ)
Yo Yo Ma, The Soul of the Tango: The Music of Astor
    Piazzolla, 1997 (SONY MUSIC)
57 Minutos con la Realidad, 1996 (INTUITION MUSIC)
Astor Piazzolla and the New Tango Sextet, Live at the BBC 1989,
    1997 (INTUITION MUSIC)

Baden Powell

Personalidade, 1987 (POLYGRAM DO BRASIL)
Live at the Rio Jazz Club, 1990 (CAJU MUSIC)
Le Génie de Baden Powell, rereleased 1990 (MUSIDISC)
Seresta Brasileira, 1991 (CAJU MUSIC)

Tito Puente

Homenaje a Beny Moré, 1978 (TICO)
Tito Puente and His Orchestra, Dance Mania Volume 1, 1958;
    rereleased 1991 (BMG)

Tito Puente and His Orchestra, Night Beat, 1995 (BMG/ARIOLA)
50 Years of Swing, 1997 (RMM RECORDS & VIDEO)
Oye Como Va: The Dance Collection, 1997 (CONCORD)
The Best of Tito Puente, El Rey del Timbal, 1997 (RHINO)

Sun Ra

The Heliocentric Worlds of Sun Ra, 1965 (ESP-Disk')
Sun Ra Arkestra: Sunrise in Different Dimensions, 1980, 1981
    (HAT HUT RECORDS)
The Singles, 1996 (EVIDENCE MUSIC)

Amália Rodrigues

Amália Rodrigues at the Olympia Theatre, 1956 (MONITOR
    INTERNATIONAL)
O Fado, 1990 (MOVIEPLAY PORTUGUESA)
American Songs, 1992 (CELLULOID)
Amália Rodrigues, 1997 (MOVIEPLAY PORTUGUESA)

Oumou Sangare

Moussolou, 1991 (WORLD CIRCUIT)
Ko Sira, 1993 (WORLD CIRCUIT)
Worotan, 1996 (WORLD CIRCUIT)

Andrés Segovia

A Centenary Celebration (box set), 1994 (MCA)

Ravi Shankar

Homage to Mahatma Gandhi and Baba Allauddin, 1981
    (DEUTSCHE GRAMMOPHON)
Concert for Peace, 1995 (MOMENT)
Ravi: In Celebration, 1996 (ANGEL)

Mercedes Sosa

De Mi, 1992 (TROPICAL MUSIC)
30 Años, 1993 (POLYGRAM DISCOS)
Gestos de Amor, 1994 (POLYGRAM DISCOS)
The Best of Mercedes Sosa, 1997 (POLYGRAM DISCOS)

Caetano Veloso

Caetano, 1987 (POLYGRAM DO BRASIL/VERVE)
Circuladô, 1991 (POLYGRAM DO BRASIL)
Caetano e Gil, Tropicalia 2, 1993 (POLYGRAM/VERVE)
Fina Estampa, 1994 (POLYGRAM)
Livro, 1998 (MERCURY BRAZIL)

Tom Waits

The Heart of Saturday Night, 1974 (ASYLUM)
Nighthawks at the Diner, 1976 (ASYLUM)
Rain Dogs, 1985 (ISLAND)
Frank's Wild Years, 1987 (ISLAND)
Big Time, 1988 (ISLAND)
Bone Machine, 1992 (ISLAND)
Beautiful Maladies, 1998 (ISLAND)

Atahualpa Yupanqui

30 Ans de Chansons, 1990 (LE CHANT DU MONDE)

Following are my desert island selections—a few CD's I'd take to play on my solar-powered boom-box beneath sun and swaying palms. This is a very personal list that will take listeners on a far-flung tour around the world. Several of these titles are imports and a few may be more difficult to locate than others, but all are well worth the effort. Bon voyage.

King Sunny Adé & The African Beats
Juju Music, 1982 (MANGO)
Synchro System, 1983 (MANGO)

Sunda Africa
Tanpa Rintangan, Tak Ada Kegembiran (No Risk No Fun),
1997 (GLOBE STYLE)

Africando
Vol. 1 Trovador, 1993 (STERN'S AFRICA)

Alla
Foundou De Bechar, 1994 (AL SUR)

Abed Azrié
Lapis Lazuli, 1996 (SONY FRANCE)

Munir Bachir
Meditations, 1996 (MAISON DES CULTURE DU MONDE)

Buena Vista Social Club
Buena Vista Social Club with Ry Cooder, 1997 (WORLD
    CIRCUIT/NONESUCH)

Sheila Chandra
Weaving My Ancestor's Voices, 1992 (REAL WORLD)

Ry Cooder & Vishwa Mohan Bhatt
A Meeting by the River, 1994 (WATER LILY ACOUSTICS)

Cornershop
Woman's Gotta Have It, 1995 (LUAKA BOP)

José Fajardo y Sus Estrellas
Al Compas de Fajardo, reissued 1994 (PANART)

Fairuz
The Legendary Fairuz, 1998 (EMI HEMISPHERE)

Peter Gabriel
Passion (soundtrack for The Last Temptation of
Christ), 1989 (REAL WORLD/VIRGIN)

Ghazal
Lost Songs of the Silk Road, 1997 (SHANACHIE)

João Gilberto
The Legendary João Gilberto, 1990 (EMI/WORLD PACIFIC)

Soeur Marie Keyrouz
Cantiques de l'Orient, 1996 (HARMONIA MUNDI FRANCE)

Ali Akbar Khan
Signature Series Vol. 2: Three Ragas, 1990 (AMMP)
Ali Akbar Khan with Asha Bhosle, **Legacy**, 1996 (TRILOKA)

Ivan Lins, et al.
Tribute to Noel Rosa, 1997 (VELAS)

Edu Lobo
Meia Noite, 1995 (VELAS)

Boy Gé Mendes
Lagoa, 1998 (LUSAFRICA)

Musicians and Poets of Rajasthan
Divana, 1996 (LONG DISTANCE)

Najma
Qareeb, 1989 (SHANACHIE)

Orchestre National de Barbès
En Concert, 1997 (TAJMAÀT/TINDER)

Rosa Passos e Vânia Bastos
Especial Tom Jobim, 1998 (VELAS)

Leila Pinheiro
Catavento e Girassol, 1996 (EMI BRAZIL)

Rachid Taha
Diwân, 1998 (BARCLAY)

Ali Farka Touré & Ry Cooder
Talking Timbuktu, 1993 (HANNIBAL)

Hector Zazou
Sahara Blue, 1992 (CRAMMED DISCS)

Collections & Compilations

30 Ans de la Musique Africaine: 1960–1990
1991 (Sonodisc)

Africa, Never Stand Still
(three CD's) 1994 (Ellipsis Arts)

Brasil, A Century of Song
(four CD's) 1995 (Blue Jackel)

Brasil, The Ultimate Collection
(four CD's) 1990 (Phonogram France)

Brasil Now
1998 (EMI/Hemisphere)

Cuba: I Am Time
(four CD's) 1997 (Blue Jackel)

Cuban Gold Vol 1: Que Se Sepa, ¡Yo Soy de La Habana!
1993 (Qbadisc)

Cuban Gold Vol 2: Bajo Con Tumbao
1995 (Qbadisc)

Dead Man Walking, The Score
1996 (Sony Music)

Desert Blues: Ambiances Du Sahara
(two CD's) 1995 (Network Medien)

Duende: From Traditional Masters to Gypsy Rock
(three CD's) 1994 (Ellipsis Arts)

Global Celebration: Authentic Music from Festivals and Celebrations Around the World
(four CD's) 1995 (Ellipsis Arts)

Global Divas: Voices from Women of the World
(three CD's) 1995 (Rounder)

Global Meditation: Authentic Music from Meditative Traditions of the World
(four CD's) no date (The Relaxation Company)

Jali Kunda: Griots of West Africa and Beyond
1996 (Ellipsis Arts)

Les Merveilles Du Passé: 1957–1975
1991 (West African Classics/Sonodisc)

Passion: Sources
1989 (RealWorld/Virgin)

Peaceful Planet: A Collection of Musical Meditations from Around the World
1997 (Mango)

Kwanzaa Party: A Celebration of Black Cultures in Song
1996 (Rounder)

Women of the Spirit
1998 (Putumayo)

Voices from the Sun
1994 (Auvidis)

Quango World Groove
1997 (Quango)

Rhythm Zone: A Collection of Dance Music from Around the World
1997 (Mango)

Tougher than Tough: The Story of Jamaican Music
1993 (Mango)

Road of the Gypsies: L'épopée Tzigane
(two CD's) 1996 (Network)

Shaman, Jhankri & Néle: Music Healers of Indigenous Cultures
1997 (Ellipsis Arts)

The Soul of Cape Verde
1996 (Lusafrica)

Sufi Soul: Echoes du Paradis
(two CD's) 1997 (Network Medien)

Voices of Forgotten Worlds: Traditional Music of Indigenous People
(two CD's) 1993 (Ellipsis Arts)

Morocco: Crossroads of Time
1995 (Ellipsis Arts)

Big Noise: A Mambo Inn Compilation
1995 (Hannibal)

The Music of Cambodia
(3 volumes) 1997 (Celestial Harmonies)

The Music of Islam
1998 (Celestial Harmonies)

Trance
(2 volumes) 1996 (Ellipsis Arts)

Collections Produced By Tom Schnabel

Quango World Voices
1996 (Quango)

Trance Planet Vols. 1–4
1995–1998 (Triloka)

Acknowledgments

For their generous assistance the editors would like to thank Jennifer Balantine/MCA, Nick Clift/Caroline, William Claxton, Chris Clunn, Carmo Cruz/União Lisboa, Hari Har, Alan Geik, Nick Gold/World Circuit, Vivienne Goldman, Juan Gomez/Harmonia Mundi, Terri Hinte/Fantasy, Sandra Izsadore, Ade James, Jumbo Vanrenen/Palm Pictures, Steve Laufer, Jesus Naranjo/RMM, Nnamdi Moweta, François Post/Lusafrica, Claus Schreiner/Tropical Music, Diana Sergi/DL Media, Robert Shahnazarian, Sachiko and Brad at *Straight No Chaser*, Stephanie Voychik at Nardulli, John Szwed, Swifty, Dominic Norman Taylor/All Saints, Hector J. Varona, Peter Williams, Ian Wright, Dan Zeff, and Daniel Zimbaldi and Timothy Kitz at Zona Productions.

	Cover illustration: Ian Wright; courtesy of Kim Evans and Dave Hucker
2	Adrian Boot; street dancer, Podor, Senegal
7	Michael P. Smith
8	Volkmar Wentzel/National Geographic; Zululand, Republic of South Africa
10	Neil Okrent; *Yemayá*, Conjunto Folklorico Nacional de Cuba
14, 17	Naomi Kaltman/Crescent Moon/Epic
18–19	Jack Vartoogian; Rubén Blades with Marc Anthony, New York, 1997
21	Silvio H. Alava/Latin Beat
23	Wolfgang Kaehler; Portobelo, Panama
24	Courtesy of Daresh-Sharq, Beirut, Lebanon
25	Arab Film Distribution; design: Rima Sinno
26, 27	Vincent Soyez/visual concept: Nuit de Chine
28	Peter Williams
31	Jack Vartoogian; Central Park, 1994
32	Stephen Laufer
35	Wolfgang Kaehler; Rio de Janeiro, Brazil
37	Geoff Crawford/Opal Ltd.
38	Richard Dean/Opal Ltd.
41	Jack Vartoogian; Asha Bhosle, NYC, 1988
42	John Colao; *Triumvir I*, Cuba Libre, 1996; right: Courtesy of Sonido/IMP
43	Silvio H. Alava; St. Nicholas Arena, NYC, 1959
45	Denis Rouvre/Lusafrica
46, 49	Eric Mulet
51	Ana Jobim; Rio de Janeiro, 1987
52	Alexander Caminada/Caroline
55	Stephen Laufer; Djivan Gasparyan (second from left) and group, Los Angeles
57	Adrian Boot
58, 59	Michael Hodgson; Los Angeles, 1998
60	Saul B. Marantz/MCA; right: I. W. Schmidt/MCA
61	Paco Manzano
63	Peter Williams
64	Editions Ennachat; lower left: Pierre et Gilles/Antoine Leroux-Dhuys/Barclay, 1992
67	Dave Peabody/Real World
68–69	Jack Vartoogian; Central Park, 1993
70	Albert Moldvay/National Geographic; Badshahi Mosque, Lahore, Pakistan
71	Robert Leslie/Real World
72	Courtesy of Columbia Records
73	Columbia Records; inset: Movieplay Portuguesa; Lisbon, 1962
74	Ade James
75	Ian Wright
77	Jack Vartoogian; Apollo Theater, Harlem, 1989
78	Ghariokwu Lemi/Eurobond/Yaba, 1988
79	Ade James
80–81	Ian Wright
83–87	Adrian Boot
88	Alain Bifot/Aldo Club
89	Christopher Clunn Archives, 1994
90–91	Augusto Brázio/União Lisboa; inset: Daniel Blaufuks/União Lisboa
93	Wolfgang Kaehler; Algarve, Portugal
94, 97	Paco Manzano
98	Michael Hodgson; Lyceum, London, 1975
101–102	Christopher Clunn Archives, 1993
104	Wolfgang Kaehler; Gorée Island, Senegal; lower right: Palace flyer, Los Angeles, 1989

Index